GW01459003

Please return this book on or before the date shown above. To renew go to www.essex.gov.uk/libraries, ring 0845 603 7628 or go to any Essex library.

Essex County Council

Pan's People

Our Story

by Babs, Cherry, Dee Dee and Ruth
with Simon Barnard

SIGNUM BOOKS

For Flick and Louise

First published in Great Britain in 2013 by Signum Books,
an imprint of
Flashpoint Media Ltd
173 Mill Road
Cambridge
CB1 3AN

A CIP catalogue record for this book is available from the British Library.

Hardback ISBN 978 0 9576481 0 4
Paperback ISBN 978 0 9576481 3 5

Editor: Marcus Hearn
Designer: Chris Bentley
Cover design: Peri Godbold
Picture research: David Pratt

Printed and bound in China by 1010 Printing International Ltd.

CONTENTS

★★★★★★★★★★★★★★★★★★★★★★★★★★★★★★★★★★★

FOREWORD

★★★★★★★★★★★★★★★★★★★★★★★★★★★★★★★★★★★★★

In the early 1970s I would often bump into Flick Colby, either in the elevator at the BBC's North Acton rehearsal rooms or the corridors of BBC TV Centre in Wood Lane.

I would be the first to bemoan the fact that I had five days to choreograph seven routines with The Young Generation for *The Rolf Harris Show*. If Flick was ever upset it would be about losing a "particularly good routine" they'd been rehearsing for *Top of the Pops* that week. The reason for the loss was because the record had dropped out of the charts. Consequently, they'd had to replace it with new choreography to an entirely different track in just a few hours.

Neither of us was going to be as artistic as we felt we could be due to the fact that we had "external pressures beyond our control." It was a well-worn excuse and we'd always end up throwing our arms around each other, laughing and parting with a friendly kiss. I know we both felt better having shared each other's problems.

It was totally impossible not to be captivated by Flick's soft American accent and beautiful face, that lit up with the biggest smile you could ever wish to see. She was truly a child of the '60s and a joy to spend time with. Whatever difficulties she faced every week, they didn't stop her from inspiring Pan's People to become the most sexy and seductive group of girls I have ever seen in my life.

Having said that, they had such class, elegance, taste and decency that, while every young man fell in love with at least one of them, they never once alienated or intimidated their female audience. Therefore, Pan's People will always be fondly remembered and admired by an entire generation of television viewers.

The book that you now hold in your hands bears testament to that fact. It is an insight into the lives and loves of each girl and a wonderful reminder of those magnificent times.

Nigel Lythgoe
July 2013

OPPOSITE:
Pan's People join
Top of the Pops –
Louise, Andi, Flick,
Ruth, Dee Dee and
Babs on the roof at
TV Centre, 1968.

PROLOGUE
FIRST STEPS

★★★★★★★★★★★★★★★★★★★★★★★★★★★★★★★★★★★★★

BABS LORD
PAN'S PEOPLE 1966-75

I always wanted to be a ballerina.

My mother was a dancer and she created a school called the Mary Lord Stage School in Aylesbury. I started going to my mum's school when I was very very small. I think it helped as far as baby-sitting was concerned, but I was always put in the back of the class because she didn't want to show any kind of favouritism. I loved dancing and thought this is really what I want to do. I suppose I started dancing when I was about four or five.

My father was in the army. He was in the Royal Tank Regiment during the war, which is where he met my mother. My mother was a dancer; she went to the famous Italia Conti school. She wanted to be a ballerina but grew too big for ballet and then the war came and she joined ENSA, the entertainment corps. She met my father – who was based in France at the time – and they married in Brussels six weeks later. That's what sometimes happened during those war years.

When the war came to an end, my father and his regiment were stationed in Germany. I was born in November 1945 and we were based in Germany for the first couple of years of my life. Then we came back to England and, after my brother John was born in 1948, Father bought two dilapidated cottages in Wendover which he converted into our family

OPPOSITE:
The 74/75 Pan's People line-up – Sue, Cherry, Dee Dee, Ruth and Babs.

9

home. My mother started her dance school to make ends meet, as my father had now come out of the army and was finding his feet on civvy street.

My mother knew dancing would be a tough life, so she was encouraging up to a point, but not pushy. I badgered her a bit to try and audition for the Royal Ballet School, but in her wisdom she said that, if I grew as buxom as she had, I would be thrown out.

The Arts Educational School, Tring Park, Tring.

So she found the Arts Educational School at Tring Park, which was only five miles away from us. It was an all-round theatrical school that taught dance, drama and music, and had a good academic reputation as well. My parents scrimped and saved to send me there. I was a day girl first, and then asked if I could board. So again, they dug deep and managed to raise the fees so that I could become a boarder.

My first professional job was when I was 12, joining the junior chorus in the pantomime *Jack and the Beanstalk* at the Palace Theatre Watford. Jimmy Perry, who wrote *Dad's Army*, and his wife Gilda ran the theatre at the time, and after the pantomime they asked me to join them in a murder mystery play which was part of their repertory season.

Every Christmas, Arts Educational supplied the children that would take part in the Royal Festival Ballet's Christmas production of *The Nutcracker*. It was performed at the Royal Festival Hall. There were two child roles: Fritz and Clara. Aged 14, I played the role of Clara. My dream as a little girl come true. Magical memories.

Aged 15, as my mother had predicted, I grew too tall and buxom for the ballet world. I left Arts Educational in Tring and joined the London branch, which was then based at Hyde Park Corner. I wondered what to do, how to take a dancing career forward. And then I thought that, as I had studied modern dance and also some drama, maybe I should explore that direction – try for drama. But learning lines I found very, very hard; much harder than learning dance steps.

DEE DEE WILDE
PAN'S PEOPLE 1966-75

All my life, since I was a very small child, I wanted to dance. It was almost preordained, because my mother – a very excitable and volatile Italian lady – was told by a fortune teller that when she grew up she would marry someone from overseas, that she would have twins and one of them would be on the stage. So when I came along my parents christened me Alida, after the great Italian actress Alida Valli.

My father was an ex-commander in the Royal Navy, DSC, retired. He was a quintessentially English gentleman; he even wore a monocle. My mother was living in Sicily when she met my father towards the end of the war. After they married in her home town of Messina the couple came back to live at Castle Toward in Scotland.

Eighteen months later they moved to England and I was born in September 1946 – and 15 minutes later out popped my twin brother Stuart. Our first years were spent in Hamburg, where my father entered the diplomatic service working for the Foreign Office. I was about three when we returned to England and it was around then that I decided I wanted to dance, so my mother took me off to ballet lessons.

Then, when I was almost ten, my parents had to find a boarding school for me because my father was going off to work in Africa. I auditioned for the Elmhurst Ballet School in Camberley, Surrey and got in. So I spent the next seven years of my life learning how to become a classical dancer.

My parents were very encouraging, but I hardly saw them because they were far away in Africa, and in the holidays I was farmed out to anybody who would have me, as going out to Ghana for school hols was not a viable proposition.

Elmhurst was full of hopefuls, young girls who wanted to learn to perform. My contemporaries included Hayley Mills, Jenny Agutter and Fiona Fullerton. The school was situated in leafy suburbia in four different buildings scattered round and about Camberley. It was very Dickensian; we had very little central heating, and when we went to bed at night I slept under the roof with icicles hanging down from the ceiling. The ballet studios were in the grounds of the main house, so every time we went to ballet class we'd have to wrap up warm as we scuttled to the freezing cold studios.

It took me about a term to get used to school and the winter climate. Living in Africa with my parents, life for my brother and me had been idyllic. Warm weather, long lazy beach days and the freedom to do what we liked. I came down to earth with a bump when I was flown back to England for my first day of boarding school. I stood shivering, all alone in a draughty common room with the rain pelting down on the large French windows.

My first term at Elmhurst was an eye-opener; learning how to cope with other girls, how to make my bed, how to deal with the cold and experiencing all the disciplines that I never had to deal with in sunny Africa. I learnt the hard way. Boarding school toughened me enormously.

I didn't really enjoy my time there but Elmhurst at least gave me a good grounding in ballet, if nothing else. My education was pitiful. I learnt nothing, nor anything worldly either. There was no sex education in those days so I left in total innocence and ignorance. I hadn't a clue where babies came from, though at the back of my mind I had a weird notion that maybe I'd come out of my mother's armpit!

RUTH PEARSON
PAN'S PEOPLE 1967-76

I remember being entranced by the ballet. My parents used to take me to Covent Garden Opera House; we used to sit in the 'gods' as these were the cheapest seats. When I was about three, I was standing in the aisle at the front of the gods, absolutely absorbed, and apparently I was trying to copy the movements of the ballet dancers. And my dad said everybody close by was watching me instead of the dancers on stage.

My parents met in Egypt during the war. My dad was a conscientious objector, and so was in the medical corps and then the educational corps. My mum, who was from Israel, helped with the nursing. Dad had to fight really hard for them to get married, because the army didn't encourage what would be considered mixed marriages. Anyway, they did marry and came over to England, where I was born in July 1946.

My dad was an artist, from a family of musicians. My uncle was a professional violinist, and I had a lot of other aunts and cousins who played the cello, piano, sang – all classical stuff. So I was a bit of a black sheep for going the more commercial route. I remember my dad wearing a beret. He was quite an artistic, free-thinking man – very clever. And very talented. When he was young he was planning to be a concert pianist, but he suffered so much with nerves that he didn't pursue it and instead followed his passion for art.

I went to the Ballet Rambert School. I won a grant from Surrey County Council, but it wasn't a full grant; my parents had to contribute. I can remember my audition very clearly. There were four people in this municipal room at a great big desk and they interviewed me. And I remember getting up and holding onto the door handle and demonstrating certain barre exercises to them. I must have been about 11, something like that.

13

It was a struggle financially for my parents to send me to ballet school. They sacrificed a lot for me, and I was very aware of that at the time and very grateful. Although we didn't have much money, my parents still managed to take me to concerts, art galleries and the ballet at Covent Garden.

I enjoyed school. My aspiration was to be a ballet dancer, but that started to change. One of our teachers taught Martha Graham's style of dance, which was very different – the basis of modern dance today. So we had one lesson a week in that, which I absolutely loved. I realised I wasn't going to be a prima ballerina and I became more and more interested in this more modern style of dance. I also began to realise that, to be a ballerina, it's 24 hours a day. It's very regimented, and there's very little room for individuality. So I was beginning to see that my personality might not fit in.

When it came to leaving, the school thought I should pursue more of an acting career – which appealed, but I refused to give up my dancing. At that time, there were very few drama schools that took dance that seriously. So I ended up going to Corona Stage School. Which I didn't enjoy very much at all.

DEE DEE

To be a ballerina you have to be of an incredibly high standard, and in my heart of hearts I knew that I wasn't. So after Elmhurst I spent a year at Corona Stage School, where I learnt modern dance.

Corona was a tough, down-to-earth school with kids from different backgrounds. Many of the parents struggled to pay the school fees but it did churn out a few good people; for instance, Richard O'Sullivan, Dennis Waterman, Judy Geeson, Susan George, plus Ruth and Louise from Pan's People.

I remember one lovely guy called Tony Villeroy, who was quite poor. I asked him, "How do you manage your school fees at Corona?"

He replied, "Oh, I go and bet on the horses, and if I do really well I come to school."

That's how it was, and woe betide you if you were even slightly posh. I arrived on my first day feeling really good in a rather smart dress my mother had bought me from Peter Jones. But as I walked into the school room and opened my mouth to say hello, I was pelted with everything imaginable by my fellow pupils. I wised up immediately. I soon learnt to rough up the edges of my vowels and melt into the background.

I enjoyed being there and learnt a lot, especially jazz dance with Ivor Meggido.

RUTH

There were some very good actors and actresses, and also some good dancers at Corona. But at the time it just seemed so irreverent and was a real culture shock for me. The other students were much more streetwise than I was, and would go off and work on film, theatre and TV jobs. They were all very talented, but I just didn't fit in. I'd been brought up in a really strict ballet environment and was just a very serious little ballet dancer.

So I used to play truant and go up to the West End, to the Max Rivers Studios, where I started studying with a choreographer called Gary Cockrell.

Max Rivers Studios was where all the professional dancers used to go. Before I eventually told my poor parents what I'd been doing, I went nearly every day, taking every chance I could. I still went to school and did the drama classes, but at every opportunity I would go up to the West End.

DEE DEE

As a young dancer looking for work, your first port of call on a Thursday was to head for the nearest newsagent and pick up *The Stage*, turn towards the back and go to the auditions page. There was an advertisement for dancers in *Sleeping Beauty* at the Wimbledon Theatre, so

I thought I'd give that a shot. I ended up not being in the chorus but was chosen as one of the four fairies bearing gifts for Princess Aurora. I was well pleased because it was my first big job and I had a solo to perform.

It was wonderful to have my parents come and see me, especially my mother. One of the first times I came out on stage, I was just doing my pirouette turns when I heard a voice shout out, "Alida, bambolina, it's Mamma!" You can imagine I almost fell off my pointe shoes as my darling mother screamed at me in Italian from the middle of the audience.

I finished the pantomime and then went to an audition for The Ronaldi Dancers, run by a man called Dudley Singleton. I got the job, which was working in a cabaret in Spain. Dudley was this strange young man who'd decided he would manage young girl dancers, but I don't know if he could manage an ice-cream van to be honest.

We drove down to this nightclub in Madrid in his car, but when we arrived there were hundreds of police milling around and sirens going off. It turned out the club was owned by the son of the mobster Lucky Luciano, and he was brought out in handcuffs and stuffed into a police van. So we'd arrived in Spain all excited about working at this club, and it was immediately closed down.

After about a week the club re-opened and we started working there. But we were constantly fighting with the management because they wanted us to sit with the customers. A lot of girls capitulated but we absolutely refused. So we became quite unpopular and decided it was time to leave.

We motored down to the south of Spain to see if we could get a job elsewhere, and by the time we arrived at Torremolinos Dudley was in such a state trying to keep a bunch of disillusioned girls happy that he developed an eye infection and went to hospital. We ended up dancing in a casino on Gibraltar, where we eventually scraped together enough money to get us back to England. Was I glad to be home!

ONE
THE BEAT GIRLS
1964-66

★★★★★★★★★★★★★★★★★★★★★★★★★★★★★★★★★★★★

RUTH

Quite a few of the other students in Gary Cockrell's class at the Max Rivers Studios were already professional dancers, working in the West End. I was a complete novice.

Gary was teaching jazz, what we now call jazz dance. He was an American actor and dancer who'd come over here with *West Side Story* in 1958. He stayed in London and decided that he was going to teach. He had a very baby face and was quite charismatic, especially in those days, being American. And the kind of jazz dance that he was teaching us… Well, nobody else did that.

Gary had formed a dance group for *The Beat Room*, which started in July 1964 and was BBC2's alternative to BBC1's *Top of the Pops*. It was meant to give the impression of taking place in a club; there was a live audience and a coffee bar and so on. The Beat Girls were Diane South, Linda Lawrence, Ann Chapman, Jenny Ferle and Lyn Wolseley, and Gary persuaded them to take me on too. I don't think, initially, they were very pleased about it. Because I was very naïve and had a lot to learn.

Anyway, we were the resident dancers.

BABS

The Beat Room was different from *Top of the Pops* in that they created it like a club, with a bar selling soft drinks, not alcohol. The BBC thought it would be difficult to get hold of major artists, but the producer, Barry

OPPOSITE:
The Beat Girls film a promotion for 'Getaway' by Georgie Fame and the Blue Flames, July 1966.

19

Langford, was convinced it wouldn't be a problem, because they'd want to be on the show to help promote their records.

RUTH

I remember my first entrance. I can't remember what the music was, but the girls dragged me on by one leg, on my bum. That was my introduction to it all. They threw me in the deep end to see if I could swim.

Everybody was learning, in fact. The cameramen, the director, everybody was winging it really. BBC2 was very much the avant-garde channel; in all spheres, drama – whatever – it wasn't about viewing figures at all. It was where a lot of real talent was developed. People were just allowed to try things out. They were trying out technical things with lighting, with scenery, with cameras, everything.

Anyway, I joined and then we auditioned Babs.

Babs as a Beat Girl at the Venice Film Festival, September 1966.

BABS

At the time I was sharing a flat in Clapham with three other girls from Arts Educational. We were all out of work and used to get *The Stage* newspaper. We always flipped straight to the back pages to see what the auditions were going to be, and I noticed one morning that there was an audition to join the team of dancers taking part in *The Beat Room*.

I thought I can but try, but it was modern American jazz dancing which I had only done a little of. I had no money at the time, but then out of the blue, the morning of the audition, I received a postal order from my grandmother which meant I could attend. I cashed it and off I toddled.

The audition was at the Max Rivers Studios

in Covent Garden. About 200 girls were applying for two places.

RUTH

I was there at the audition, at Max Rivers. Everybody was shocked by the amazing response – 200 girls.

BABS

I'd been an all-rounder, really – drama, modern, tap. But when Gary gave us the sequence to learn for the audition, my hair stood on end. I thought, "I'll never learn that." However, as we were gradually whittled down, I found myself in the final bunch.

Sitting there with Barry Langford and Gary Cockrell was the floor manager Jim Moir, who would later become producer-director of *Top of the Pops*. And it was Jim, apparently, who said, "Pick the blonde one. I like her smile."

So, to my absolute astonishment, I was picked – with a girl called Jo Cook. Unfortunately Jo was already contracted at the time, doing nightclub work at the Savoy and the Talk of the Town. So she backed out and it ended up being just me.

I suppose you could say it was Jim Moir who changed the course of my life.

RUTH

We had a weekly slot and it was mainly frantic jazz dancing. We saw a video of it recently, and it was so fast I thought it'd been speeded up. I said, "Did we *really* move that fast?"

This style of dance had never been seen on television before. Even within the British dance world, there was nowhere to train in the modern style of dance. American jazz was very new.

Light entertainment at the time was very straight-laced, people forget. It really was still very much in the 1950s. Dancers on television were *The Black and White Minstrel Show*, The Tiller Girls… It was the old-fashioned line-up, high-kicking, hair up in a bun, that sort of thing. That's why our hair came down and was free-flowing, which was unheard of at the time. That was really like not wearing a bra. It was naughty, naughty.

BABS

We had one costume which was hipster jeans down to the knee, sneakers, socks and then little red tops with our names across the front. I had pigtails and one of the girls had bunches; it was early 1960s rock 'n' roll. Routines were very fast and jazz-based, and all very new to me.

The Beat Room didn't have the same kind of rules as *Top of the Pops*. Anything went. If Barry liked the artist, and the artist was in the country and wanted to be on the programme, then they were on the programme. Barry wanted to get the top-notch people. He had The Rolling Stones, Eric Clapton, Jimi Hendrix, Tom Jones, Lulu, The Moody Blues and The Animals to name just a few.

Barry was so un-BBC. He popped purple hearts and polo mints one after the other. I was in the *Beat Room* studio when The Who came in and smashed up their instruments for the first time. Drum kits went flying, guitars were getting smashed; it was electric stuff. I remember Barry running down the steps from the gallery. We all froze, thinking, "Oh my gosh, this is terrible. Barry is going to go crazy about this."

And he came screaming down into the studio saying, "This is fantastic! Can you do it again?"

RUTH

It was Gary's gig. The choreographer was the king pin. And he just auditioned whomever he wanted as dancers. He could have fired any one of us and replaced us.

BABS

If we hadn't been on *The Beat Room*, we could well have been called The Gary Cockrell Dancers. To all intents and purposes, we *were* The Gary

Cockrell Dancers.

After the first six months of *The Beat Room*, Gary and Barry decided to change the concept of the programme. Ann Chapman left and joined The Younger Generation, and we were joined by a girl I'd also been to school with, Carlotta Barrow. Her nickname was Zooks.

The Beat Girls with Georgie Fame promoting his number one single 'Getaway' in July 1966.

Gary and Barry liked the name Zooks so they decided they'd name the next series *Gadzooks! It's All Happening*. It was going to expand on what *The Beat Room* had been – to make it more theatrical. And we moved to a bigger space at Riverside Studios.

That's where we met The Beatles for the first time, when they came on the show. I remember being very brave and knocking on their dressing room door just to say hello. They were charming. I wish now I'd asked them for their autographs, though perhaps it would have been a bit un-cool.

RUTH

After the show, we all used to go downstairs to a VT room and watch it. I remember sitting on the floor in between The Beach Boys. One of them was reading *The Joy of Sex*, and I went out and bought it to find out what he was reading. And I remember Tom Jones being on the show, when he did 'It's Not Unusual'.

BABS

He was very shy. I was sitting at one of the tables when he came in to do his rehearsal; he was wearing black jeans and a black t-shirt and had these long black curly locks. I sneezed and he said, "God bless you." And then suddenly he launched into 'It's Not Unusual'. Everybody stopped and thought, "Ooh. Wow. This is amazing." I seem to remember he had his lucky mascot attached to his belt, a rabbit's foot. It certainly brought him much luck – that and his incredible voice of course.

So over the next nine months – on *Gadzooks! It's All Happening* – we threw away the jeans and the tiny tops and Gary's imagination went a little crazy. We did strange, interesting things. I remember being painted black for one routine. We wore loin-cloths and tattoos and strange hair, which was very innovative for the time. And Ruthie and I did a duet to one of my favourite tracks at the time, 'The House of the Rising Sun' by The Animals. We wore these sexy blue lace mini-dresses slit up the sides.

RUTH

I loved that. A pale blue lace dress with slits up the side. We were meant to look like whores from an old American whorehouse.

BABS

In September 1965 the BBC decided they didn't want *Gadzooks!* any more and we were dropped. We then had a pretty lean 12 months or so, during which Gary got in touch with a Dutch television company. A producer called Bob Royens was doing an equivalent pop programme, not dissimilar to *Gadzooks*, in Amsterdam – at Hilversum, the television studios there. And he was looking for some interesting avant-garde ideas for his programme, which was called *Moef GaGa*.

RUTH

So we used to go over and do *Moef GaGa* once a month, which hardly paid our rent. We were very very poor in those days.

BABS

While we were doing *The Beat Room* and *Gadzooks*, Gary also decided that he was going to create a dance centre. So he bought an old banana warehouse in Covent Garden, in Floral Street, and called it the Dance Centre. He was able to pay for it because he managed to get the BBC to rent it for us to rehearse in. And that rental helped develop the studios that they became. So we were now rehearsing in this old banana warehouse with a little chap called Cliff, who was a carpenter and was building up these studios around our ears.

RUTH

It was dangerous. I mean, it wouldn't be allowed now. And he made us rehearse at weekends, Christmas, Boxing Day…

BABS

It was cold, dire. And we all put up with it to help Gary create the centre. It was all part and parcel. We were doing the shows in Holland, then Gary got us a gig working in a discotheque in Bond Street, a club called the Drum.

RUTH

They had glass drums with lights underneath and we'd just have to stand there and boogie. Sometimes only one or two people would come in. We were paid £3 a night. It was so demoralising, but we needed the money. I hated it.

BABS

Meanwhile, Gary's ideas were expanding and expanding. He had this notion that he wanted groups of Beat Girls as cheerleaders at football matches. He wanted them in nightclubs, he wanted them performing internationally around the world – and his idea was that we could go off and train up teams.

RUTH

The first time I met Flick Colby was at the Dance Centre, in reception. She was beautifully dressed and she sat beside me. And we just started chatting.

It was a terrible winter; she was living in a freezing cold flat and was finding it difficult to settle down. She'd come from a quite obviously wealthy background. She asked me where she could buy Charles Jourdan shoes – these very expensive French shoes. So I told her where Bond Street was, and we used to joke that we bonded over a pair of expensive shoes.

Another shot of The Beat Girls' 'Getaway' promo.

DEE DEE

Flick came from Pennsylvania, from quite a wealthy family. One of the places she trained was the Joffrey Ballet Company, one of the most prestigious ballet companies in America.

Flick had wonderful technique. And she didn't have to work at it – I had to work at it. She had a natural ability and a natural sexuality when she danced. She had this beautiful, heart-shaped face, but there was a sort of naughty glint in her eye.

BABS

Flick had arrived from America in January 1966 with her first husband, Robert Marasco. Robert was going to the London School of Film Technique and they were due to be here for a year. Flick had trained in New York in dance – modern and ballet – and as soon as she got to London she looked for a place where she could continue to take classes.

And that's how she came to the Dance Centre. There was a coffee bar and juice bar, and we met her there and we became friendly. We were just generally chit-chatting and told her we were unhappy about the situation we were in with Gary.

RUTH

We were so unhappy, in fact, that three of us – Jenny Ferle, Lynn Wolseley and myself – walked out on The Beat Girls and started up our own group. We called ourselves Tomorrow's People.

DEE DEE

Because in those days there were so many dancers and so little work around, I'd decided that I would go out and find myself a job. At the time there was a famous fashion store in Kensington called Biba. It was the creation of designer Barbara Hulanicki and her clothes were absolutely the trendiest things to be seen in; every young girl in England wanted a Biba dress. I decided that if I couldn't find work as a dancer then the next best place to work was Biba.

I went for an interview and got the job straight away. Working there was wonderful because you rubbed shoulders with all the stars. One day I was working behind the reception desk when in came this diminutive but very pretty lady with an American accent and long brown hair. We were all allowed to wear outfits from the shop, and on that day I was wearing a light suit which was basically a tight little jacket and a short skirt with a flare at the bottom, in a pink diamond motif pattern. It looked great on me.

This particular customer went all round the store and then came back to the desk and approached me.

"Oh hi," she said. "That outfit you have on, I would like one just like that."

"Madam, have you looked around?" I said.

"Yes, but I couldn't see one."

"Well then, I'm afraid I'm really sorry but we haven't got any more."

To which she replied, "Well then, I'll just have yours. Who is the manager here?"

Stephen Fitz-Simon, who was Barbara Hulanicki's husband, came out and this lady said to him, "Listen, I've been talking to your young assistant here. I want her outfit."

And he said to me, "Dee Dee, go to the changing room and take it off."

I was absolutely astounded. I was so cross. But I did what I was told. I went and took it off and wrapped it up, still warm. She said, "Oh, thank you so much, Mr Fitz-Simon," and he sort of bowed.

And that's how Raquel Welch walked off into the sunset with my dress suit.

Anyway, around this time I was sitting on a bus, halfway up the King's Road Chelsea, and reading the audition page in *The Stage*. There was a big advertisement in the middle and it said Gary Cockrell was auditioning for The Beat Girls on Friday the 7th of May 1966.

So on Friday morning I arrived at Biba and went to the manager, clutching my mouth, and said, "Fitz, I'm really sorry, but I have a terrible toothache and at two o'clock I've made an appointment to go to the dentist."

I'd already had an agonising time the day before, going through my wardrobe so I could find the most fitting outfit to wear the next day. I actually found a top which was a sort of neon light orange – if you had a hangover you'd probably keel over at the brightness of it – and I thought if I wore that maybe I might stand out.

There were between 200 and 300 girls at the audition, and in the large studio in front of the mirror sat Gary Cockrell, owner of the Dance Centre, his partner Valerie Hyman, a pretty girl called Flick Colby with long brown hair, a rather beautiful tall girl with very blonde hair called Babs, and Diane South, who was Gary Cockrell's choreographer.

We were all crammed into the room; there were so many girls there my bum was being imprinted onto the back wall. Diane came out and started teaching us the routine, and of course being right at the back I couldn't see a thing. So I thought, "Come on Dee Dee, you've got to do something about this," and pushed and elbowed my way to the front. But I was so nervous that picking up the steps was almost beyond me. I remember Diane saying, "You, the girl in that very bright top – everybody is going that way, and you're going the other way."

I realised at that point that if I was going to get through this audition then it wasn't my dancing but my personality that would do it. I put on the most brilliant smile I could and whenever I went wrong I just laughed it off. And Diane kept saying "You, you and you can leave..." And miraculously I was still there.

Towards the end there were only a few of us left, and then at one point it was just me.

BABS

I remember her audition well. There were hundreds of girls there. I think she was wearing an orange top, green tights and about three or four pairs of knickers. Dee Dee always seemed to wear about three or four pairs of knickers in those days. And she had her hair up in a ponytail, and a big smile. She was radiant.

LORELLY HARRIS
PAN'S PEOPLE 1966-67

My mother was a dance teacher and I started very early. I got a scholarship to the Royal Ballet School at the age of 11. When I got to the Upper School, I was a student in Barons Court and they were pushing me to be a soloist. But I was very tall and my back gave out.

So they said, "Why don't you try jazz?" I promptly tried to learn jazz and went to the Dance Centre, where Gary Cockrell was holding forth. And he asked me if I'd like to be part of The Beat Girls. So I thought, "Why not?"

It was May 1966. I was the youngest; I was just out of ballet school and I didn't know what I was doing. I was quite hefty and I was trying to get my head around acrobatic jazz dance. I was trying to learn to bend my legs rather than straighten them.

We'd rehearse at the Dance Centre all night. It was when Covent Garden was still a market, and we'd go out afterwards and there'd be these open-front wagons with tea and bacon sandwiches. So at four o'clock in the morning we'd be drinking tea and eating sandwiches with the porters in the market. We'd work all night and then get a train or a bus or a plane somewhere to start work.

It was a very exciting time for everybody. It really was the beginning of everything. And don't forget, in those days, the pill was just coming out. It was all peace and love and liberty, and it was all coming to a head.

Anyway, in September The Beat Girls went to the Venice Film Festival for the film *Fahrenheit 451*. It was me, Dee Dee, Babs, Flick, Diane South and Penny Fergusson. We were there as the cabaret for the opening of the film.

BABS

I remember we had little white t-shirts with the logo of the film on the front. We had little red mini-skirts and white boots, which we had to wear on the flight over to Venice. In those days, the rules on air traffic procedures weren't as stringent as they are now. And we were invited into the cockpit of the plane in pairs to meet the captain.

When it was my turn, I went into the cockpit with Lorelly. And the captain just looked at Lorelly and his eyes kind of glazed over. Lorelly was beautiful – very tall, long blonde hair, long legs. And he asked if I'd like to sit in his seat. I think it was so that he could talk to Lorelly.

The Beat Girls fly Alitalia to the Venice Film Festival.

And as I was chatting to his co-pilot – this is an Italian airliner, by the way, Alitalia – he said the plane was flying on auto-pilot. And I said, what was that? And he showed me. He took it off auto-pilot and said, "The plane is yours." We were flying over the Alps at the time, and he let me hold the controls for a few minutes and then he put it back onto auto-pilot. Bearing in mind we'd forgotten about the fact that there were 350 passengers at the back of the plane… And then we were taken back to our seats.

We came in to land in Venice and were picked up by a launch and taken to where we were going to stay, at the Excelsior Palace Hotel on the Lido. It was that evening that we were going to do our cabaret, with the singer Lulu's backing band, The Luvvers.

After we did the cabaret, Penny Fergusson and I heard that there was a party going on hosted by the film director Roger Vadim. And we decided we were going to gatecrash it. So we headed off to the room where it was being held and sneaked in. We hid behind a curtain, looking at all the very glamorous people – the film stars and everybody drinking champagne. And somebody spotted movement behind the curtain and pulled the pair of us out and made us dance. So we did a kind of free style dancing.

All huge fun.

LORELLY

We were staying in a hotel on the Lido, where all the stars were. The actor Peter McEnery was just down the corridor from us. Babs, with great aplomb, invited him to have tea in our room. It was very funny. When I think about it now, we were so flipping innocent. We were totally naïve, all of us. We'd just come out of ballet school and, in actual fact, there was quite a nasty scene at the Venice Film Festival.

BABS

At one point a film producer who had spied Lorelly took her off for a drink. He'd taken over a suite on the ground floor and Lorelly had vanished into these rooms. And we had to go and get her out. We decided she'd been in there a little too long.

LORELLY

I received a message to say there was a press call in room such-and-such and, like a twit, I duly went and knocked on the door of room whatever-it-was. And the door opened and there was the film producer Raymond Hakim in his silk dressing gown with it all hanging out.

I nearly had a heart attack. I was only 17 and hadn't really seen an old man's bits and pieces before. It was horrifying. And he proceeded to chase me round the room. So having got to the other side, I leapt over the bed and rushed out of the door. Then I had a complete nervous breakdown.

BABS

We eventually got her out. It was a whirlwind. It was heady. It was just a crazy time. We were chased down the beach by paparazzi, we partied, we drank bellinis and we danced. I don't think we slept at all during the 48 hours we were there.

LORELLY

Back in London, we had a whole gang living in Earl's Court, in what was called Kangaroo Valley. We knew all the people from RADA; we knew all the people from St Martin's and the Royal Ballet. And so many of those people made it. In fact, one of my girlfriends from ballet school was two doors down and was living with Joanna Lumley. Jo had spots, so when she had to go modelling we'd spend hours making up her spots so the camera wouldn't pick them up.

BABS

But by the end of 1966 we were becoming more and more demoralised. Nothing was happening. We didn't want to train girls for Gary's new groups of Beat Girls. There'd been an audition to join a wonderful choreographer called Paddy Stone, who was putting together a team of dancers for the first Tom Jones series at ATV, and I'd got the job and was thrilled. But Gary said I couldn't do it because I was contracted as a Beat Girl. So I was even more unhappy.

DEE DEE

Gary approached us in December and said he wanted us to do a gig in Bournemouth, over Christmas, for £7-10s each. He was adamant that he wanted us to do it. But we said to him, "There's no way we're going to Bournemouth over Christmas for £7-10s."

To which he replied, "If you don't do it, then you can forget about The Beat Girls."

"That's fine," we said. "We're walking out."

So we did.

Flick was renting a room in a flat in Earlham Street at the time. So Flick, Babs and I ended up in Earlham Street, sitting there most of the night – it was December the 8th – and trying to work out the name of the new group we were going to form. Flick was going to choreograph us and we were going to depict in dance what was happening in the music scene at the time. Trying to find a good name took forever. After quite a few bottles of wine, we really couldn't come up with one we all liked.

BABS

Everything we came up with sounded like a rock band. Flick came up with the idea of something Greek. The Dionysus Darlings. We managed to persuade her against that one. And then I think it was me who said, "Who is the god of dance – dance and music?" And Flick, I think, came up with "Pan." And we thought, "Pan… That's got a nice musical ring to it."

DEE DEE

I do remember Dionysus Darlings going out of the window in the early morning.

And then somebody mentioned the fact that Pan was the god of dance and music and debauchery and everything else. He was a bit of a naughty boy. He had six handmaidens and, as the legend goes, used to hide behind a rock while they were bathing and then jump out, which sent them into a panic.

It was Flick who eventually said, "I know. Let's call ourselves Pan's People."

BABS

Back in the summer The Beat Girls had been asked to take part in a promotion for Georgie Fame's record 'Getaway', which involved a Getaway toy, like a Frisbee. And the man who was organising the publicity side of it was James Ramble; he'd been in the RAF, had quit and got into PR.

When Pan's People started we didn't actually go out to look for a manager but James said to us, "I can help you." He was interested in the concept of a dance group. It was new. It was innovative. It hadn't been done.

DEE DEE

When we sat up that night in December and decided on the group name, it was also agreed that James should be our manager.

He was a very personable chap. He was tall, with a thatch of orange hair. He stuttered and was quite funny as well. He and Flick were seeing each other; in fact, they subsequently got married, briefly. He seemed very astute and keen to help us. And we did need some kind of guidance, somebody behind us. On our own, it would have been very difficult to have managed ourselves. We owe an awful lot to him. He went out and did his utmost to try and procure work for us. I don't think we could have done it without James.

He lived on the top floor of 73 Duke Street in the West End of London, round the corner from Selfridges. So when Pan's People got together we congregated for a meeting in his flat to discuss how we were going to make Pan's into the greatest dance group ever. That's kind of how it started.

BABS

To make the group up to six we brought in Lorelly Harris and Penny Fergusson, plus another girl called Felicity Balfour... And then we set out to get work for Pan's People.

TWO
PAN'S PEOPLE
1966-67

★★★★★★★★★★★★★★★★★★★★★★★★★★★★★★★★★★★

DEE DEE

The first Pan's People gig ever was in December 1966. It was around the 21st, in Belgium.

They only wanted two girls and the fee was about £8 each. So to decide who was to go we all drew straws. Lorelly and poor Babs drew the short straw. They went over to Belgium and did the gig and came back with their £8 each and shared it amongst all of us.

We'd already decided that any monies we made were going to be split between us. Whatever gig, whatever job came in, to keep the group going, we shared everything.

LORELLY

Jim sent Babs and me to a fairly sleazy nightclub in Liège. We got our train tickets and neither of us really spoke French, but we got there in the end. There was an English band there too, and we decided, rather than come back by train, we'd come back with the guys in their van. And there we were – Babs and I – making sandwiches in the back of the van, when it seized up right in the middle of a great plain in the middle of Belgium. It had run out of water.

BABS

I leapt out of the van to knock somebody up and get bottles of water to put in the engine. We did, eventually, from a farm, and topped up the

OPPOSITE:
Pan's People 1967.
Back: Lorelly,
Penny. Front: Dee
Dee, Babs, Flick,
Ruth.

37

radiator with water. Eventually seeing the white cliffs of Dover from the ferry was such a relief. I remember the chaps dropping us off somewhere in London. How I got home, I don't know; we were absolutely exhausted.

DEE DEE

Christmas came and went, and when we got together in January 1967 James had landed us this amazing job. It was for a TV series in Belgium called *Vibrato*. And the station wanted a troupe of dancers to host the show.

At that time the music scene in Britain was absolutely incredible. Britain was the mother of all pop music; we ruled the world, what with bands like The Beatles and The Rolling Stones. Everybody wanted to know what was happening in Britain. Countries like Belgium, Holland and Germany had their own pop shows, but most of their pop groups were pretty dire. So the British groups used to go abroad to promote their songs. The money was also much better over there, both for the bands and for us.

Each girl was paid £45, which was a fortune. And on top of that we got £30 a week for food. We used to save this and live on chips and mayonnaise for the week. When we got back to England we needed the money to survive during the lean times. It was absolutely essential to keep the group going.

We did Belgian television every single month and stayed in Brussels for approximately a week. It was always the same thing. The TV company would put us on a flight first thing in the morning, so there would be six bleary-eyed girls arriving at six o'clock to catch the first plane out. Our accommodation, the Hôtel de Boulevard, was in the sleazy part of Brussels. Many a time when we exited, all dolled up to go filming, men would throw money at us, which we'd pick up and save for the pot.

The director was called Leo Quollin, a typical Gauloises-smoking Frenchman. He always had a cigarette hanging out of his mouth. He was very French; stocky, smoky eyes, short spiky hair. And then there was

Pierre the producer. I think he was really into Babs, but she definitely wasn't into him. He was a large-nosed, skinny Frenchman who was incredibly excited about having Les Pan's People Girls on his arm. He'd always try to escort us everywhere.

The very first show we did was on the 8th of January 1967. We were all terribly excited about our new job, and visiting Brussels. This TV show had saved our life; at last, we were going to be earning some money. It was about eight o'clock at night when we landed on Belgian soil and I remember us all chatting and saying, "I wonder what the hotel is like... Can't wait to go and have a lovely meal and see a bit of the city. Maybe they'll take us to a bar or a disco or something."

The excitement was incredible.

But it was freezing cold in Belgium, and also knee-deep in snow. And – unfortunately – we weren't dressed for the Arctic. Leo was there to meet us with Pierre and a minibus. So we all piled into this minibus, comforted by the thought of a hot meal and a nice glass of wine. About three quarters of an hour into our journey we thought, "Hold on a second. Where are we going?" It finally dawned on us that we were deep in the Belgian countryside heading for God knows where!

Nine o'clock... Ten o'clock... Finally, at 11 o'clock, we arrived in the middle of absolutely nowhere. We entered a large house to be confronted by hundreds of spotty-faced adolescents between the ages of ten and 15. It turned out that this was a boarding school for the children of factory workers. We stared at them and thought, "What the hell are we doing here?"

We soon found out. Leo came over and said to us in broken English, "We film here. Tonight. Now!"

Meanwhile all the boys – who had obviously been deprived of female company – closed in on us, so Leo took command and escorted us to the changing room: the boys' lavatory. When we came out in our costumes, mini-skirts and skimpy tops, there were cheers and whistles and lewd gestures. And we just thought, "My God. What have we come to?"

And then one of us saw a group standing around, with their instruments. It was Ray Davies and The Kinks. Some British faces, thank God for that! This cheered us up a little bit.

Then Leo said, "OK. Rehearse ze number, we're going to film it here." We said, "What number?"

Somehow we managed to get some steps together to back The Kinks and filming went ahead.

It was about 2.00 am when six very weary dancers climbed back into that minibus. That was our first experience of Belgian television. But it got better. We did many OBs – outside broadcasts – in some lovely places. There was always an awful lot of standing around, not understanding what anyone was saying, while the Belgians stared at us and raised their eyebrows. But the series was a life-saver for us. We did Belgian TV for about three years.

Taking a break during filming in Belgium.

BABS

Flick was becoming more and more creative. And the show gave her a great opportunity to be experimental.

Because she was choreographing and creating the camera scripts, designing all the costumes, and trying to get the concept through to the production team in Brussels, we decided it would be better if a member of the group flew over to Brussels and delivered the camera scripts.

I was the one who was nominated to take the scripts over. I used to do a day trip – fly to Brussels and meet with Leo Quollin. We would have lunch. I'd show him the script, describe Flick's ideas and the designs for the costumes, so that it was all ready for when we flew over later to record the show. I loved that part. I felt like a businesswoman almost – with my little briefcase with all the scripts inside. It gave everybody an opportunity to get an idea of what Flick, technically, was going to do.

Vibrato was very forward-thinking technically. They'd created this video machine which could edit almost on the spot, which gave enormous freedom to the kind of work Flick was wanting to do. It meant her imagination could go crazy. It was like filling in a jigsaw puzzle. We might do the same routine three times, but we would only do sections of it. And those would be recorded. And then we'd go back and fill in a bit more while recording. And then we'd go back and do a little bit more. That was very innovative for its time.

I quite enjoyed the technical aspects and used to sit in the gallery with the vision mixer, the chap that used to actually press the buttons. I'd give the cues for the camera changes and enjoyed that enormously. So I probably didn't do as much dancing in those shows as the other girls, but I didn't mind because I was still part and parcel of the team.

LORELLY

We just wanted it to be a success. And we worked very hard. I can remember coming back from Brussels. We'd worked so much and so long, I think I absolutely crashed out for 36 hours. Jim Ramble was sending out telegrams because nobody was answering the phone. I was OK afterwards. And I hadn't taken a pill or anything. I just was so tired, I had to recuperate.

DEE DEE

As we became quite famous in Belgium, other TV shows started to come in. We worked a lot in Amsterdam for VARA Television; firstly on *Moef*

GaGa, a pop show, and then other shows for famous Dutch entertainers like Johnny Rec and Herman Van Veen.

On top of this we did the odd gig as well; one festival we danced in featured Johnny Halliday and Françoise Hardy, big stars on the continent. But we didn't really get any work in England. So for the first 18 months of Pan's, most of our dancing life was spent abroad.

BABS

I looked after the costumes; they were in big trunks and I had to make sure they got to the gigs.

There was one occasion when we were flying off to Belgium to do a show. I arrived at the airport and met up with the girls, but I'd realised in the minicab going there that I'd left one of the costumes at home. Fortunately my grandmother was able to put the costume in another taxi to Heathrow. We were about 40 minutes away, so I said to everyone, "Sorry, but it means I'll probably miss this flight. But I've checked and I can get the next flight."

Dee Dee went absolutely cold. Flick asked what the problem was and she said, "I had a dream last night that Babs left a costume at home, and we went on the plane without her and the plane crashed."

Flick said, "Fine, no problem – you can come on later with Babs, so that will break the dream."

So Dee Dee stayed with me and the girls went on first with one load of costumes. We followed on the next flight out 40 minutes later.

LORELLY

When we were doing *Vibrato* in Belgium, we had all the big French stars appear on the show, like Claude François. He was a huge star in France, but he died very young after trying to change a light bulb while he was in the bath; it didn't agree with him. After that we called him Mr 100,000 Volts.

I remember when he appeared on *Vibrato* we danced on a canal barge while he was singing. And that's where he got the idea for his own backing group, The Claudettes. He realised that it was a good idea to have a load of ladies bumping and grinding behind you when you're singing. In fact, Pan's People were the start of nearly all the French artists who were coming up at that time, employing six go-go dancers behind them.

DEE DEE

Most of Pan's really gelled as a group, but it became increasingly obvious that Felicity Balfour really wasn't happy and didn't want to stay. So she left, and Ruth joined us in March.

RUTH

Jenny and Lynn and I weren't really getting anywhere as Tomorrow's People. After walking out of The Beat Girls we rented a little church hall near my parents. We went there every day to rehearse and contacted as many people as possible trying to get work. We'd worked in Holland and Belgium in The Beat Girls, so we had contacts there. And, through those contacts, we got several TV gigs out there.

But it was tough, because it was a new concept to hire a group with their own choreographer. People weren't going to take that on. They were still following the old concept: you hire the choreographer, then they use their dancers.

We lasted about 18 months. And then a job in Israel was being offered to just two people and the two other girls accepted it without even discussing it with me. They told me, "We accepted the job. That's the end of Tomorrow's People."

I was disgusted, quite honestly. So I just phoned up Flick, because we'd been friends in The Beat Girls, and said, "Have you got a job for me?"

I replaced Felicity Balfour. I was the newie. And I don't think I fitted in very well at the beginning, because I joined on condition that I'd be able to do some choreography. Obviously Flick wasn't very happy about that, but I presume James, our manager, twisted her arm.

I can remember going to Holland and going into one of the girl's bedrooms and they were all in there. Something must have been going on, business-wise or something. But it all stopped the moment I walked in. I was a bit lonely at first. I remember sitting with my book of poetry in the coach, on my own.

DEE DEE

So there we were. Flick, Babs, myself – the original founder members – plus Lorelly Harris, Penny Fergusson, a very sultry, sexy girl with ginger hair, and Ruth. So that was the six Pan's People.

Maurice Béjart, from the Béjart Ballet Company in Brussels, had seen us on *Vibrato* doing a number where we were all in a row, lifting our arms and legs in time to the music, and was very impressed by how tight we were. Somehow he got hold of James Ramble and suggested that, while his company was on vacation that year, would Pan's People step into their shoes?

We started work on the show in April. It was a new opera, *Gulliver*, composed by Gui Barbier and commissioned for the King and Queen of Belgium. We were chosen to be the resident dancers in this particular opera, which for us was absolutely amazing. It was going to be performed at the Cirque Royale in Brussels, which originally had been a circus. In actual fact, our dressing rooms, which were in the bowels of the earth, were the original lions' dens.

It was a very strange set-up. Having been a big circus ring, there were vomitoria off to each side, like side-pieces of the stage, so you could hide behind them and suddenly appear. But the set or performance stage, instead of being a solid floor, was only grids. There were paths you could walk or dance down, and move around – paths forward, to the side and diagonal. And in between these were mesh grids, with the orchestra underneath us! Also, it was very dark and we couldn't see. So most of the time we were terrified.

We'd come out to dance on these paths in the pitch black, knowing that

A typical 1967 publicity pose.

one false move would land us in the lap of the bass player, or even on the head of the poor conductor. On top of this, we were very aware – with our incredibly skimpy costumes – that the orchestra could peer up our knickers!

RUTH

Lorelly is very tall and blonde and I'm small and dark. We were great friends, but an odd couple height-wise. Anyway, it's traditional, at the end of a show, for the dressers and technicians to play jokes on you. We had a quick costume change into this all-in-one costume, and the dressers swapped my costume for Lorelly's and vice versa.

The costume change was so fast, we had no option but to wear them. Lorelly squeezed into my costume but couldn't possibly get it done up properly, and mine was floating about because it was far too big. And I just remember, we were opposite sides of the auditorium – in the round – coming up the vomitories for our entrance. Everyone, including us, was laughing so much. We were crying with laughter. It must have been quite a sight.

BABS

It was, as we were told, a 'political, satirical farce'. It used opera singers from all over the world and a 75-piece orchestra, which was double-tracked and intermingled with electronic music. So it was a very avant-garde piece.

The routines we did were also very avant-garde. We did what was called a can-can. But the can-can was, in fact, not a can-can at all; more a token gesture to a can-can. We wore Mary Antoinette wigs and white costumes – white leotards, little white skirts, white lace suspender belts, white stockings and little white shoes.

DEE DEE

Our costumes were amazing. They were styled very much in the Aubrey Beardsley fashion. The first costume we had was all in white with these funny peaked hats, white stockings with suspender belts and shoes, and white bodices cut extremely low, just above our nipples.

On the opening night we came out and did our first number. At the end of the routine, as a finale, we'd run down these strips of wood and jump into the splits, arms up in the air. My strip of wood was right in front of the royal couple. As I went into the splits, my hands and arms went up in the air and out popped my bosoms, right in front of the King of Belgium. He got an eyeful, but I don't think he was complaining.

BABS

In the meantime, while we were doing the shows in Belgium, we were also flooding the BBC Light Entertainment department with scripts, with photographs, with all sorts of ideas about this new and innovative dance group that they should employ.

DEE DEE

Then James Ramble came up with another coup. As The Beat Girls we'd done the first series of *The Dickie Valentine Show* back in July 1966; now James had managed to get us into the second series as the resident dancers. So around August the 11th our first show started, over at ATV in Elstree; the shows went out on Friday evenings at about 8.25.

Working on British television was absolutely amazing. In those days, back in the 1960s and '70s, the family variety show was all the rage. Family entertainers like Dickie Valentine, Norman Vaughan or Bruce Forsyth would have their own show where they'd perform their own songs, have backing dancers, a live band and a couple of guest artists.

I can't remember if it was on *The Dickie Valentine Show* or his own show when Tom Jones was in such tight pants that he split his knickers. He was doing that all the time though. Tom was very well-endowed, back and front, so it was inevitable that he would part company with his tight trousers. Much to our delight, of course.

Around the same time, on the 31st of July, James got us a three-week stint at the Savoy Hotel. The idea was that while everybody was sitting in

The camera script for the third show of the second series of **The Dickie Valentine Show,** *recorded on 17 August 1967 and broadcast eight days later.*

Posing with Dickie Valentine on 28 July 1967, the day Flick married Jim Ramble.

the very smart restaurant, drinking champagne and eating Cordon Bleu food, we girls would come out and dance our routines. It was a thankless task, because nobody really bothered to watch and nobody really bothered to clap.

The hotel built us this long catwalk, with a stage at the end, in one of their main dining rooms. We'd make an entrance trying to look slinky and sexy, ready to dance. But we had these ghastly costumes, purple leotards and tights, and on top of our heads, for some ridiculous reason – I still don't know why to this day – were plonked different-coloured ringlets made of raffia which had been lacquered down. Bright pink, fluorescent orange, luminous green… Totally ghastly. I think the diners probably choked on their steak béarnaise as we came out.

BABS

I remember getting in cars and racing down from the Dickie Valentine recordings to the Savoy. Initially we were allowed to walk through the front entrance – until one night when we were terribly hungry and picked up fish and chips en route. We walked through the lobby of the Savoy eating fish and chips and were asked to use the tradesmen's entrance after that.

One of our routines was to 'Summertime'. We wore purple cat suits – purple tights and leotards. It was quite a classical number, a very hard routine actually, that Flick gave us to do. And while we did this, all I remember was the clatter of plates and people talking, and me thinking, "They shouldn't be allowed to eat while we're actually dancing."

It was soul-destroying, really. What they really wanted were plumes and feathers and fishnets. I suppose it was ill-judged on our part. We thought we'd bring art and culture to cabaret, but I don't think it went down at all well. People didn't want art and culture.

DEE DEE

On the 26th of August we went back to Belgium to do another show.

There was something in Belgium called the Golden Sea Swallow of Knokke competition, in which different television companies competed against each other for this very prestigious award, like Belgium's answer to the BAFTAs. Knokke was the Belgian equivalent to Brighton or Blackpool and was permanently raining and foggy. I don't ever remember being at Knokke when there was any sunshine.

I *do* remember, after we finished the gig – we didn't win – we all got on a coach together and went back to Brussels. Status Quo were on the same bill, and The Moody Blues too, doing their hit 'Nights in White Satin'. So it was absolutely amazing being on this bus with these two famous groups; one of those nights that you just don't forget. We were laughing, telling jokes, having fun, singing all the way back to Brussels.

I bonded in particular with Rick Parfitt and Francis Rossi from Status Quo, and we were always friends with the Moodies from then on. I had the most enormous crush on Justin Hayward, but he never looked at me. He wasn't interested. I pined away!

BABS

In the early days, James Ramble, our dear manager, thought, "I can save some money. I'm going to buy the girls their own transport."

He found a 1956 green Buick, like one of those big gangster cars. And we had a trunk containing all our costumes – a massive trunk which would go on the roof, with us in the back of the Buick, my brother John driving and James in the front.

Flick, in the meantime was saying, "Well, you can all do that, but I'll use my own money. I'm going to fly."

RUTH

She was sensible.

BABS

But somehow we all managed to squash into this car. Our first little adventure in the Buick, in October 1967, was to drive to Brussels and then to Madrid, for cabaret. We got half way to Dover – it was very early in the morning – when the vehicle gave up the ghost.

We pulled into a service station, got on their phone, and managed to find a lorry that had the particular part the Buick needed. Then we drove on down to Dover. I remember driving through Dover High Street when Ruth suddenly said, "I don't feel very well." Down went the window and Ruth threw up on Dover High Street.

RUTH

I think I'd had a fun time the night before.

BABS

We managed to get onto the boat and went across in a force nine gale. We were down below at the bar drinking, and it was a very long crossing. John was terribly sick. Ruth was sick again.

RUTH

I was sharing a bucket with Babs' brother; it was that bad. Almost everybody was sick. Very few were still standing.

BABS

We'd put into another port because the weather was so bad. Then, when we eventually arrived – an hour and a half late – everybody was sick, tired and emotional. We went below to get into the Buick, John turned on the ignition and – nothing. Some of the crew helped us push the car off the boat and to the top of the ramp, and then left us.

While we stood there holding it, as we were so nervous about it rolling back, John managed to find a phone and call the equivalent of the French AA, who came out and fixed the car. But they said, "Whatever happens, don't stop until you get to your destination. Because if you do, the car will pack up again."

RUTH

Also, the French customs took the Buick apart. Because it all looked a bit weird; all these girls, great big case, you know. We must have looked a bit hairy and beatnik-y to them, I suppose.

BABS

We managed to get to Paris. We found a little pension. And we were so exhausted. Next morning, to our amazement and relief, the car started. We drove. We got as far as Tours and the car gave up the ghost again. This time we left my brother with the car and got the Trans Europ Express from Tours to Madrid. Luxury.

It took John three days to sort out the Buick. He dumped it in the back streets of Tours, managed to hire a Peugeot estate from Hertz and three days later came and found us in Madrid.

DEE DEE

After that terrible journey we ended up in Madrid in this sleazy nightclub. It was absolutely awful. And not only was it awful, we also had a long walk to get to the stage, which was so vast we looked lost in such a large space. On top of that the damp permeated everywhere; we had water on the floor of our dressing room and rats as well.

LORELLY

God, that was dingy. The dressing room was carved out of the earth and it was dank and dark and there was a naked light bulb hanging from the ceiling.

BABS

The Spaniards wouldn't let us wear our costumes. We were checked every night before we went out on stage when we did the club. We weren't allowed to show our belly buttons.

RUTH

We spent all night sewing on strips to cover up our bare midriffs.

BABS

The other singers and dancers would have their tummy buttons covered, but their boobs were pouring out. I mean, they were wearing g-strings. But their culture was, you can't show your belly button.

DEE DEE

And then we did a gig at the National Stadium of Madrid. There was a cycle track with cyclists peddling furiously, round and round. And right in the middle of it was an arena, like a boxing ring, where we performed. There were thousands of people in the audience. Thousands. I don't know

The group's ill-fated gig at the National Stadium of Madrid.

how they saw us; we were like specks in the distance. Because of the crowds we had to have police protection from the eager public. But, in fact, we needed protection from the police, because they kept pinching our bums.

RUTH

And we never got paid. We didn't fulfil our contract, because we were all so ill. In the end, James just said, "We're packing up and going home."

BABS

We thought that was the last we'd see of the Buick. Weeks and weeks went by, and then one morning I woke up and looked out of the window of my parents' house in Barnet and thought, "Oh no, what's that?" It was the Buick. It had been brought back by the AA on a trailer and dumped outside the house where it was registered. John managed to get it to the local dump, but again it came back!

I had a photographer friend called Nicky Wright, who said he had a friend who loved American cars and they'd take it off our hands. We said, "We warn you. The car isn't drivable." The engine block had cracked. But Nicky said, "Don't worry. We'll manage. We'll get it started."

So they came to the house in Barnet and they got it started. It took them 30 hours to get the car down to Surrey. But they did it. And that *was* the last we ever saw of the big green Buick.

DEE DEE

We did a couple of shows in Germany for a well-known director called Mike Lekkerbush. The programme was called *Beat Club*. He used to have all the British bands come over to Germany to be on the show, and he used Pan's as backing dancers. But it wouldn't be the whole group; it might be just the three of us.

Before one particular show in Germany, Lorelly, Penny and myself were rehearsing our dance routine when suddenly a group of scruffy individuals burst through the door – led by a swaggering young man called Roger Daltrey. The band was The Who. We took a break and spent quite a bit of time chatting to them, and they were very cheeky and tried to chat us up. But we were in the middle of a rehearsal so eventually we had to tell them to bugger off so we could carry on working.

But I'll never forget that moment. These classic groups were everywhere and we, as dancers, were getting to meet them. It was every girl's dream to meet The Beatles, The Who, The Rolling Stones and so on. And we were part of it – the most iconic era of music that ever was.

RUTH

Although we did work, we had to pay for our rehearsal rooms, costumes and so on. So really we were being kept by our parents. Every little bit of money we earned went back into the group. It looked like we would never break into England, because people just wouldn't take a unit like us – a group with their own choreographer.

BABS

What you need is someone who is out there pushing for contacts. We wrote to every head of every television station in Europe. We banged on doors constantly – for about a year I suppose. It was hard going. But, after 12 months, Lorelly and Penny decided that it wasn't going to work and that they wanted to leave the group. They just lost faith in what we were doing.

DEE DEE

Louise Clarke joined us in December 1967 and Andrea Rutherford joined two or three months after that. James found Andi. Louise was just 18; Andi was 20. They'd both previously been in Ivor Meggido's Jazz Group.

BABS

They fitted in very easily: lovely girls, bubbly and fun. And good dancers too.

RUTH

We all got on very well and had a lot of fun. Andi was a great dancer. Louise was very easygoing; nothing fazed Louise.

DEE DEE

She was always, always late. I was always, always on time.

I remember Louise's very first gig, when we went on the train from Brussels to Zurich to do a TV show. It was Christmas time. We were on the platform, trying to get on this train with hundreds of Belgian and Swiss people with skis. We were dodging skis the whole way to Switzerland.

James always came with us and sorted out the monies. Most companies paid you in cash. That was fantastic for us, because when we got to the airport we could go to Duty Free and buy Christmas presents for our parents and boyfriends. That money was crucial to us.

But when we quit the hotel in Zurich to go to the airport, James left all the money from the gig in the drawer of the hotel room. It was probably about £45 each, which was a lot in those days. We didn't find out about this until a long time after. Flick gave us all our money at the airport. It was only years later that we found out Flick had used all of her own money to pay us, so that we could buy our presents and wouldn't be disappointed for Christmas.

LORELLY

At the beginning of '68, I had a bust-up with my man of the time. I had to get out of London, and quite by accident I went along with a girlfriend who was auditioning for the Bluebell Girls. And as always, when you go for moral support, you can be sure that it's always going to be you who gets chosen and not the person who really wants it. And that's what happened.

So I was offered a very good contract at Le Lido in Paris and my poor girlfriend wasn't. It wasn't very fair. But I thought, "Right. I'll get out of London. I'll get away from my ex."

And that was that.

I think my mother was happier to see me working in Paris. Her attitude was, "I didn't send you to the Royal Ballet School for you to end up go-go dancing in the backwoods of Belgium." It just seemed like a more solid contract. It was a bit come and go with Pan's People; you never knew quite where your next job was coming from.

I arrived in Paris just in time for the student riots. I thought, "Oh, this is fun." They were throwing paving stones and turning cars over, and they put pickets in front of Le Lido. So I couldn't go to work. Then I got picked up and put in prison. I had to phone the head of Le Lido to say, "Can you get me out? I wasn't doing anything bad, I just happened to be with a load of young people. I couldn't get around them."

So they sent me home for three weeks until things calmed down.

When I got back, I ended up as line captain of the girls and ballet mistress at Le Lido. Then I became a soloist and helped with the choreography. After that I was running the stage side at Le Lido for Ms Bluebell. And when I finally got fed up with that, I was modelling and flying all over the world to present fashion shows.

Coming back from Japan one time, I met my future husband, so I ditched everything when I was about 30, got married, went to live in the south of France in Carcassonne, had twins and brought them up on a farm in the south-west of France. Then when the twins left home, I left home too, because I was fed up. And I went to the Pays Basque, where I am now.

BABS

Penny and Lorelly were only with us for a year. Lorelly went off and joined the Bluebells. Penny went and married a Greek chap and ran a pub in Notting Hill Gate.

Sadly her marriage didn't work out, but she stayed in touch with Ruth, who suggested she do the make-up course at the BBC. Some years later I bumped into Penny in Hampstead and she was working on *Doctor Who* as a fully fledged make-up artist. Louise and I were by then married with kids, so Penny invited us to bring the children to the BBC to see her at work and meet the Daleks. I remember Louise's son Tony freaking out at the monsters and wanting to leave.

It was a nice opportunity to catch up with Penny. But then we lost touch with her again. I do wonder where she is now.

THREE
A LEG IN AT THE BBC
1968

★★★★★★★★★★★★★★★★★★★★★★★★★★★★★★★★★★★★★★★

DEE DEE

1968 was the most significant year for us. It was the year that we landed *Top of the Pops*.

There was a lovely dilapidated hotel near Covent Garden called the White House Hotel, owned by an ex-RAF commander called David. When you went into the lounge, there were hundreds of old dears and old gents reading their papers, rattling their tea cups and rustling their *Daily Telegraphs*. And across the road from the hotel the Commander hired out the annex, which was large enough for us to do our rehearsals in. It was perfect, because any old dears that lived in that building were so deaf they couldn't hear us anyway.

It was the early spring of 1968. We'd just come back from Belgium and were rehearsing when the Commander came across the road and popped his head round the door.

"Hello, girls," he said. "Just thought I'd let you know that Virginia Mason is auditioning in the main building tomorrow. And she's looking for two girls. See you later." And off he went with a cheerful wave.

Virginia Mason was the regular choreographer for *Top of the Pops*, and the regular dancers were called The Gojos. We looked at each other and thought, "My God. How fantastic."

So we all decided that we'd go to this particular audition, not collectively but as individual dancers. And off we went. The next day, at the end of the audition, Virginia Mason picked two girls from Pan's

People. The two girls she picked were Ruth Pearson and myself.

RUTH

We were there for just the one show. So, funnily enough, the first number that we ever did on *Top of the Pops*, on the 4th of April, was not with Pan's but The Gojos, dancing to 'Simon Says' by The 1910 Fruit Gum Company. We hated it. But we did it purely as a ruse to get to talk to somebody and ask them to come and see us. To see if we could *all* get on *Top of the Pops*.

DEE DEE

Top of the Pops producer Colin Charman, whose other credits included **The Generation Game** and **The Dick Emery Show**.

We thought we could get a leg in at the BBC. Then while we were there we could talk to the BBC bosses or talk to the directors to see if they would take on Pan's People instead.

We'd just finished a routine with The Gojos when through the door walked this diminutive man who looked a bit like Charlie Drake, called

Colin Charman. Now I didn't know Colin, but Ruthie did. Colin was one of the director-producers on *Beat Room*, so when he walked through the door the first thing we did was pounce on him.

We propelled him to the BBC bar, pumped him full of drinks, and then at the appropriate moment said, "Listen, we've got this fantastic dance group called Pan's People. Please please would you give us a chance one week?"

RUTH

We told Colin all about our group and begged him to come and see us. It was all very new to be a group and have your own choreographer. The Gojos were still following the old format of choreographer and dancers. Colin agreed that we'd be on standby if a record had dropped out of the charts or an artist was unavailable.

DEE DEE

And that was it. We left. We carried on rehearsing for the show in Belgium, and then one day the phone rang. It was Colin.

He said, "Just thought I'd let you know, I need three dancers for the show tomorrow. Are you interested?"

Well of course we were! We were beside ourselves with excitement.

We decided that Ruth and I should do it because we knew the layout, having done one show already. Also, as Flick was the choreographer and one of the dancers, it was a good idea that she should do the show too. But we only had one day to rehearse a routine for 'Cry Like a Baby' by The Box Tops. So we took the steps from our Belgian routine for Aretha Franklin's 'Respect', rearranged them and – hey presto – a new dance. It was the 18th of April.

RUTH

For that first performance on *Top of the Pops* I was terrified. It was Dee Dee, myself and Flick. It was in Britain, it was live, and we'd had hardly any time to rehearse. That was the nature of *Top of the Pops*, which of course we learnt to deal with in time. But I think we did it quite well, considering.

DEE DEE

The powers that be liked us enormously, but we heard nothing. And then, some time in May, Colin rang us again. He said he wanted all six of us to come on *Top of the Pops* to do 'US Male' by Elvis Presley. So that was the first time that we appeared as the whole team on *Top of the Pops* – on the 30th of May 1968.

Of course, it was totally nerve-wracking because *Top of the Pops*, at that time, was live. If you made a mistake or you fell flat on your face or your teeth came out or your wig fell off, roughly 17 to 21 million people would see you.

I'm afraid that, the moment we came on the scene, The Gojos vanished into oblivion. Virginia Mason was a very reputable choreographer and she'd got The Gojos the gig, but they were no competition for us really. I remember the Gojos costumes that we wore on that first *Top of the Pops* – white culottes. I think there's nothing less sexy than women wearing white culottes. They were cut at the knee like long shorts and we had white shirts right up to our necks and, I think, white shoes or boots. We looked like ice-lollies. Every little bit of flesh was covered, except for the knees downward.

And the dance style was very typical of the 1960s: hands on your hips, wiggle from side to side, wave your arms in the air and shake your head madly till it almost comes off. That was basically it.

We brought something much more earthy, much more raunchy and sexy. We were very aware of our bodies and so was Flick in the way that she choreographed us. There was an enormous sort of warm sexiness about us. So we brought something new and exciting to *Top of the Pops*.

RUTH

Our dancing was very different to The Gojos. Although we were all technically trained – in ballet and modern dance – Flick took a lot of her style from the way kids were dancing in the clubs. So they could relate to what we were doing. And the clothes as well. She was very influenced by what was in fashion, and we'd wear what was in fashion. Maybe just a bit more extreme.

DEE DEE

Colin soon started to use us regularly. Every couple of weeks he'd ring us up and we'd do another number. So by the end of 1968, we were doing quite a lot of television for the BBC.

The Belgian gigs carried on. But now they were kind of worked out around *Top of the Pops*. Back in February, we'd done another opera, *Die Fledermaus* by Johann Strauss. This time it was at the Théâtre Royal de la Monnaie, Belgium's equivalent to our Royal Opera House. The director decided he wanted us to dance a Scottish jig over crossed swords in full Scottish tartans. We all nearly sprained our ankles and Louise actually did!

But we loved doing the two operas. I think because the costumes were always amazing and there was no expense spared. And working in a theatre – especially a theatre that had an incredible history and atmosphere – was particularly rewarding.

Between doing *Top of the Pops* and doing the show in Brussels, Flick had started up a friendship with a really wonderful director at *Top of the Pops* called Stanley Dorfman. Stanley and Flick really hit it off artistically; both were very intelligent, creative people. And Stanley was just about to start a new series for BBC2 called *Bobbie Gentry*.

STANLEY DORFMAN
PRODUCER, TOP OF THE POPS

I was one of the original co-producers of *Top of the Pops* when it started in 1964 with Johnnie Stewart. Pan's People happened when the show moved down to London.

Coming to London and going into colour, the show became a much more important thing. I think the secret was that the whole family watched it; the kids watched it for the records and the music, the mothers watched it to see how everybody was dressed, and the fathers watched it for Pan's People. I mean they were incredibly sexy, but not in a salacious way. So it became a family show.

Whoever it was who was producing that week – Johnnie Stewart or me – they directed the show too. So we had complete control over what was going to go on and would book the acts. Flick would just stand by, waiting at the telephone, and we'd call and say, "I'm afraid it's Jim Reeves." And she'd go away and then come back with a Jim Reeves dance. She always took the record seriously; she didn't mock it or take the piss out of it.

Even if it was Jim Reeves.

The brilliance of Flick Colby was that she was able to get the information the day before we did the show, and in just a day she would choreograph it, dress it, get the clothes made and do the show. It was uncanny. I don't think a group has ever been that efficient, and the dancing was always impeccable.

She was brilliant.

CHERRY GILLESPIE
PAN'S PEOPLE 1972-76

Stanley was always Flick's soul mate, no question. They spoke to each other all the time and were in contact right up to her death. Stanley knew that Flick was capable of doing much more than just choreographing *Top of the Pops*. He was a fan of hers and knew she had all sorts of ideas. He thought Flick could have been a great director.

BABS

After meeting him through *Top of the Pops*, Stanley became our mentor within the BBC. He felt that we really had something to offer, something different. So whenever he did any of his shows, Stanley persuaded the BBC to use us as dancers on the programme. We did a series with Jack Jones, which Stanley directed. We did a series with John Denver, which Stanley directed. And it was thanks to Stanley that ultimately we were allowed to have our own *In Concert* show.

DEE DEE

Anyway, Stanley had been commissioned to do a series with an American singer called Bobbie Gentry, who was famous for her song 'Ode to Billy Joe'. She looked like a Texan showgirl. She had a Southern drawl and was very tall and slim, with lashings of long dark hair and false eyelashes like brooms. She looked a bit like Louis XIV. Stanley brought her over to do a series and, of course, because he and Flick were in cahoots he said to her, "I'd like Pan's on the show and I want you to choreograph it."

So the six *Bobbie Gentry* programmes were a fantastic opportunity for us. Because not only were we doing *Top of the Pops* every now and then, but now we actually had a series too. It started in July and was great fun.

For the first time we had two boys with us, Gary Downie and Adrian Le Peltier. They were very different. Adrian was very beautiful and looked like a curly-haired Dirk Bogarde. And Gary had a very interesting long-chinned face and a great sense of humour. For Flick it was wonderful, because she basically had carte blanche to do whatever she liked.

Usually, everything on *Top of the Pops* was very restricted. In fact, working for the BBC and working for *Top of the Pops* was a bit like being at boarding school, or being in the army. There were rules and regulations about what you could and couldn't do. And the directors were God, basically. You had to do the number they wanted; whether you liked it or not was irrelevant.

But with the Bobbie Gentry show, and Stanley as director, Flick was suddenly working with somebody whom she admired and had a mind like hers, creative and inventive.

BABS

Bobbie was a sort of Southern belle. She seemed very nice to me, but was rather starry I think – a little bit precious and pampered. She was certainly very beautiful, but I don't think she was a natural dancer.

DEE DEE

She never knew what she was doing and was basically a nightmare. She could sing, and was easy on the eye as long as you didn't go in too close. She didn't like us a lot. Sometimes you work with artistes who are very outgoing, fun and inclusive, but others make you feel like you're just the dancers. I think Bobbie felt threatened by us; we were the competition. So

Performing an umbrella routine on the **Bobbie Gentry** *show with Kenny Lynch and Harry Fowler.*

she used to make sure that most of the time we were put in the most hideous outfits.

BABS

I remember the horrific multi-coloured wigs we had to wear, and getting the impression that we couldn't be as glamorous as Bobbie Gentry. She was a very glamorous lady. You never saw her with a hair out of place, you never saw her without her make-up. I think she was persuaded by Stanley that we would complement her rather than compete with her. We certainly couldn't compete while wearing multi-coloured wigs!

RUTH

She didn't like us. My abiding memory of her was that she did everything she could to make us look ugly and horrible. I remember one week, I think we were doing the song 'Sweet Caroline'. I'm very dark-skinned, and she put me in a bright yellow curly wig. I never forgave her for that. I don't think she liked competition. Plus, dancing was not her forte – basically she had two left feet.

DEE DEE

Bobbie would come out and balls up most of the numbers. For one number we were all dressed as trees. The idea was that Bobbie would sidle up to one of us and we'd wave our arms about in acknowledgment, and then she'd go on to the next tree and do a bit more.

It was all choreographed exactly to the music. But with Bobbie it all went in one ear and out the other. At one point, you could actually see her forgetting to go to the trees at all, so the trees could be seen moving across the set trying to get behind her. It looked like the trees were chasing her.

RUTH

Well, it was utter chaos. She just didn't know where she was going. We were chasing her around, it was hysterical. It was a magic forest, I think. Except it wasn't too magic for her.

DEE DEE

In between doing *Top of the Pops* and other shows, we started to do a lot of cabaret. We needed the extra money because the BBC paid so badly. We literally got the minimum amount of money, about 19 quid, which was about half of what we used to get when we were abroad doing Brussels or Amsterdam. So we used to go off and do cabaret gigs.

At that time, all around the country there were cabaret venues like the Talk of the Town in London, the Beachcomber in Birmingham and Pantiles of Bagshot. They weren't exactly discos; they were somewhere between a disco and a nightclub. There would be a big stage and people would sit at rows of tables to eat and watch whatever show was going on. Some, like the Talk of the Town, were enormous places. Others were smaller, more clubby.

That particular September, we went up to Birmingham to do cabaret at the Beachcomber with Tom Jones. He was the star and we were the guest girl dancers. In hindsight, if we'd known what it would be like, we wouldn't have gone. Because first of all, when we came out, there were only women in the audience. Not a single man, just screaming women. They actually booed as we came out, which was off-putting.

BABS

We were supposed to be the warm-up act for Tom Jones, so as you can imagine it was pretty much an all-lady audience. We weren't too popular on that occasion, because all they wanted to do was see their idol and throw various garments at him. They didn't want his stage being shared by any other young women.

RUTH

In those days, you didn't dance to recorded tapes, you had live bands. Well, musicians like to have a drink, and this particular night they got absolutely pie-eyed.

So we went on, and half the band played one number and the other half played a different number with different time signatures. Half of us were trying to dance to one number and half the other, and quite understandably we collided and had to stop the performance. The musicians were sent off for a lot of black coffee.

We stayed in a theatrical B&B that they put all the Beachcomber artists in. The landlady's name was Mrs Lovesey, and she was very strict – she didn't like us coming in late. John, Babs' brother, was there too, because he'd become our driver for a while. I was sharing a room with Flick, but there was one night when some of us had come in late and I didn't want

to disturb her, so I went to share with Babs. But John was there too, so it was the three of us in one bed, sort of like sardines.

I mean, nothing untoward happened. He was like *my* brother too. But when Mrs Lovesey came into the room in the morning she was absolutely horrified!

Andi, Louise, Flick, Ruth, Babs and Dee Dee on the roof at TV Centre, 1968.

DEE DEE

The Christmas *Top of the Pops* was completely different to the rest of the year. Usually *Top of the Pops* was based on the Top 20, but at Christmas it was made up of all the Number One records that had appeared during the past 12 months. And the track they decided we should dance to that first Christmas was 'The Good, the Bad and the Ugly' by the Hugo Montenegro Orchestra.

For some reason, Flick remembered the famous scene in *Goldfinger* where Shirley Eaton was killed by being covered with gold paint. So – not that she was trying to kill us off or anything – Flick thought, "What a good idea. Let's paint all the girls gold."

We had to have a doctor and a nurse on hand, in case we fainted or became ill. And not only were we painted from top to toe in gold, we were also dressed up as Red Indians. We had wigs on, I think, and bands around our heads. I cannot tell you how dreadful we looked. It wasn't one of Flick's better ideas.

Anyway, during our rehearsal that Christmas, it so happened that Prince Charles was a guest at TV Centre. They took him into the *Top of the Pops* studio to see us rehearse. So there we were, up on this podium and looking our worst, and the heir to the throne – who'd just turned 20 at the time – was standing about 30 yards from us. Because we were in the middle of rehearsals, we couldn't get off our podiums and say hello. And by the time the routine had finished he'd gone, which was such a shame.

But someone – I don't how this happened – someone telephoned the press to say that we'd attacked Prince Charles and caused all sorts of problems. We found out eventually that it was one of The Bee Gees playing a joke on us.

RUTH

I'd just treated myself to a really beautiful white cashmere jumper. We had loads of showers afterwards to get the gold paint off, and then I put on my jumper and went up to the bar for a drink. Then I realised I was getting very hot, and my cashmere jumper was going green. My poor cashmere jumper never recovered.

Glamorous life, isn't it?

OPPOSITE:
Babs and Dee Dee become golden girls for the Christmas edition of **Top of the Pops***, 19 December 1968.*

FOUR
TOP OF THE POPS
1969

★★★★★★★★★★★★★★★★★★★★★★★★★★★★★★★★★★★★★★★

DEE DEE

In 1968, as well as doing *Top of the Pops*, we'd done a programme called *The Golden Shot* – a game show on ITV with Bob Monkhouse. We did the *Beat, Beat, Beat* series for Hessischer Rundfunk, a series called *Top of the Night* in Ireland and a network special called *Go-Go Gig* for Air TV in Brussels.

But by Christmas of that year we'd started getting a lot of fan mail, and I think the BBC realised that Pan's People were becoming an asset to *Top of the Pops*. So it was decided in 1969 that we would be contracted to the BBC.

It was around that time, just before Christmas, that we started work on the *Happening for Lulu* series. It was transmitted from the 28th of December through to the following March; there were 13 episodes. Lulu was great. Working with her was enormous fun, because she was very infectious. She sang wonderful songs, she was a laugh, and she was very approachable. And not only did we back Lulu, but very generously Stanley Dorfman, the director, gave us our own slot on the show.

BABS

The Lulu series was very innovative. It was in one of the major studios, it could have been TVC8. And the studio was pretty much taken up by the Johnny Harris orchestra, so we were given a stage even smaller than a *Top of the Pops*-type stage to do our routines on.

So Stanley and Flick decided that it was fine to do backing stuff with another artist in the studio but, for our actual routines, we would be

OPPOSITE: Liphook filming, 25 July 1969.

73

Flick sits by the camera during a break in filming at Liphook.

filmed out on location. And, again, this hadn't been done before. We used to rehearse a routine and then film it on location. We filmed on VT, and the VT was then edited as film.

We only had a small film crew with us; a lighting and sound engineer, a director, Flick and the camera operators. I seem to remember we changed in the back of their van.

DEE DEE

We'd be in either a bus – usually a minibus – or sometimes we'd have a car to take us to these places. It'd be all of us and sometimes Tessa Watts-Russell, our choreologist. She was the girl who wrote down all our routines.

The very first one we did was at the Royal Festival Hall, and it was to a song by The Times called 'People'. I remember we filmed once in a quarry, and did another one at the Questors Theatre in Ealing. And we also did 'Tap Turns on the Water' by CCS at the Metropolitan Water Board building, an enormous place out on the A316. It was all glazed green tiles and incredibly hot. For some reason, Flick had put us in woollen jumpers and woollen trousers. God knows why she did that.

BABS

We did a rather bizarre routine on Wimbledon Common, in the mud. We did one on rooftops. We did one out at Ascot race course, but the night before there had been snow so the routine went a bit bye-bye, because it was very difficult to do a pirouette in two feet of snow. We filmed mostly in the evening, or at night. We were all huddled around the generator most of the time, trying to keep warm, before being dragged away to do a little bit of something.

DEE DEE

We had some wonderful filming days. Some of the locations weren't much fun, especially when we were freezing cold. But we did some really creative performances.

One of the most famous moments on *Happening for Lulu* was when Jimi Hendrix appeared on one of the last shows. Jimi was supposed to do his two numbers at the end of the show and then the credits would roll. But this was about the same time that Cream split up. And Jimi decided to just carry on and play 'Sunshine of Your Love' in tribute to Cream. This caused enormous problems on the floor, because instead of stopping – and Lulu then saying good night and thank you to everybody – he didn't.

We'd just been backing Billy Preston and, because the show was live, we couldn't actually get off our podiums. We had to stay there because we would've been in the way of the cameras. So we were standing there, a few metres away from Jimi Hendrix, watching this whole scenario unravelling.

The floor manager rushed upstairs to the gallery where the producer, Robin Nash, was. And then Robin came tearing down the steps, about three at a time, and rushed up behind the cameras, waving frantically at Jimi to stop. And Jimi Hendrix just put his hand out and put one finger up and carried on. All live on TV. We girls were in hysterics.

STANLEY DORFMAN

Top of the Pops was all about the Top 30, so people tuned in to see who was going up and who was going down. We compiled the charts from the radio Top 30, the *New Musical Express* and *Melody Maker*; the aggregate was the BBC chart. We had really strict rules that only records moving up in the charts, or that were static, could be played. So even if The Beatles or The Rolling Stones were Number One, and they dropped to Number Two, and we had them booked for the show, they had to be cancelled.

PAUL SMITH
FLOOR MANAGER, TOP OF THE POPS

Johnnie Stewart created the show in Manchester. It started on January the 1st 1964 and was originally intended to be just a short series; half a dozen programmes or something like that. He was charming, and one of the few people to have a personalised logo on the end board when his name came up. It was him sitting on the stool with his jacket thrown over his shoulder, and it would sit beside his name. He was a gentleman.

STANLEY DORFMAN

Top of the Pops was originally filmed in Manchester in a converted little church hall. We used to fly up, get the charts, work on the show, do the show, then fly down again. In those days it was all lip-synced. In fact sometimes we had the same band that played for everybody: if you had The Kinks playing, you might have Ray Davies singing and then some of The Kinks and some of The Who playing in the background, in the dark, and then they'd switch around.

The weather in Manchester isn't in any way conducive to pleasant living, and there was one week where half of the people just didn't appear.

It was very hairy because we never knew who was going to turn up. When Television Centre opened and the show came down to London it was just a fantastic relief. It also became very exciting, because that was when we could get dancers and an orchestra and the whole thing.

DEE DEE

So January 1969 started off with a bang. We were now doing *Top of the Pops* every week.

PAUL SMITH

I first worked on *Top of the Pops* in 1969 as an assistant floor manager. At that time the show was the most powerful way of promoting pop music in Britain. A play on *Top of the Pops* and an appearance on *Top of the Pops* pretty well guaranteed instant and immediate success. The record companies would put a lot of their resources into securing an appearance. It was getting audiences of about 12 to 14 million, which, compared to modern-day audiences, is astonishing.

STANLEY APPEL
PRODUCER-DIRECTOR, TOP OF THE POPS

I was producer and director on *Top of the Pops* for quite a few years. Prior to that I was production manager on it, and if I think back further I was also a cameraman on the programme. So I go back quite a long way.

One of the reasons for having a dance troupe on the programme was because there weren't very many videos at the time and, when we got records from foreign artists who weren't in the country, we had to have a method of visualising the record. We'd give that record to Flick Colby and she'd then have to think up a dance routine.

BABS

Johnnie Stewart was the grand-daddy of the pop world, though I don't think he had very much time for dancers at first. He saw the show as being about artists and bands. But eventually he was persuaded that, when he couldn't get hold of an artist, dancers were necessary.

We always had to dance to a record that was climbing in the charts, as it was one of Johnnie's ground rules when he created the programme that the records had to be climbing. Obviously we needed a bit of time to rehearse but the shows were recorded on a Wednesday and were broadcast on a Thursday night.

Flick would be in touch with the producers and the production office, and there would be a big debate as to which records they thought would go up that week. They'd decide on a record and then we would rehearse it.

STANLEY APPEL

There was quite a lot to do. As well as getting the dance sorted out, there were the costumes for it, the set for it and, if we had an orchestra in the studio, there had to be a score done for the musicians.

The interpretation of the song in hand was solely down to Flick. You'd meet her with the record you'd chosen, and she'd listen to it and digest it. We'd then get a designer down to see her in the Pan's People rehearsal room, and also the costume designer, and they'd sort out the set and costumes. In the period when we had Johnny Pearson and his Orchestra, the record would also have to be given to somebody to do a score. Then we all met up again on Tuesday to go to outside rehearsals.

Whoever was producing or directing the programme would go along to see how things were getting on, sort out any problems, and plot out the camera scripts. It would then have to be given to the office, so it was all typed up into a script ready to go into the studio on the Wednesday, when we used to do the recording.

No one knew who was going to be on the programme till Monday morning. At 8.30 we'd have a meeting in the office, and all the record company representatives would come along and whoever was doing the programme would read out the running order of the programme. That was the first time the record companies knew whether their group or artist

Andi, Louise, Dee Dee, Babs, Ruth and Flick take part in a camera rehearsal for **Top of the Pops.**

was going to be on the programme that week.

When that running order came out, the people concerned immediately rang up their record companies to either increase the volume of records coming out of the factories or stop them. Because if the record had suddenly gone down, they had to stop the presses producing hundreds of thousands of singles. In those early days the sales of records were enormous, they really were.

BABS

Then the chart would arrive, and we'd all huddle round the phone, with all fingers and toes crossed, in our grotty rehearsal room somewhere in Shepherd's Bush. If the record went down it meant that we had to start from scratch. So we'd put three days' work into a routine and the camera scripts and then suddenly we'd have just a day to rethink the whole routine. In the meantime, we also had costume designers who'd been working with Flick to create the costume to go with the dance routine. That used to be quite hairy, because on Wednesday we'd be in the studio recording it.

DEE DEE

We'd have to change and do a completely new number. Sometimes people used to write in unkindly and say, "Pan's People don't know what they're doing." But we'd only had half a day to rehearse something.

CHERRY

We went through a terrible time. The public pay-phone would ring in our rehearsal room, an awful working men's club, and it would be the BBC saying, "The charts are in, girls. I hate to tell you this – you're not going to believe it. It's gone down. We're biking over the new single."

We'd have to stop what we were doing. Flick would throw the single across the room like a Frisbee, then we'd wait for the new single to arrive. I used to call them Flick's Frisbees. That would mean completely different costumes in a day, a completely new routine in a day, and the set would all have to change too.

Once we had a run of about seven or eight weeks of that. It was bizarre. Whoever was choosing the singles at that time was obviously not doing a very good job!

STANLEY APPEL

On Wednesdays we would start rehearsing at 10.30 in the morning. We rehearsed up until lunchtime. Each pop group would get between half an hour and 45 minutes to do their camera, sound and lighting rehearsal. That's not long, because you'd have to get the group on stage, sort out their positions and then the lighting man had to light them.

I personally didn't like miming; in most cases when I was doing it, the vocals were live, so the sound would have to be sorted out too. We'd sort out the camera shots, the group would then go away, the next group would come on and this would happen all morning and through part of the afternoon.

SUE MENHENICK
PAN'S PEOPLE 1974-76

Rehearsal time was a free-for-all. If you were lucky you got 20 minutes. If the design team hadn't finished, they were still building sets. The lighting people were always fiddling and fussing around for ages. The bands were supposed to come in; you'd have to allow for them being late. They weren't previously scripted, so the cameramen used to be guided by a producer upstairs. So that would all take a bit longer than our routines would do.

We'd normally be in the dressing room by the make-up area and sit there until we were needed. The bands would all be called for their rehearsal time. They'd do their rehearsal and they'd go. Then the next lot would be called in.

And then, in the late afternoon, there'd be a dress run. And again, that would be stopping and starting occasionally because cameras would be in the wrong place or they suddenly realised when they put it all together that it wasn't working the way it should. So, certainly by that point, it was get out there, do your routine and that's it. And it doesn't matter if you fall over. Tough. And then at seven o'clock, the audiences were brought into the studio and it was the real thing.

RUTH

We were in Studio 8 most of the time; sometimes Studio 1. Through the years, I think we worked in near enough all of them. The dressing rooms were downstairs, in the round bit. We used to get lost a lot, but at least you could keep going round and you'd get there eventually.

Wrapped in silver foil for a late 1960s publicity photo by Frazer Wood.

SUE

When you'd actually see the show going out, it looked bigger than it was. You'd see the cameras zoom into something, and then the audience would all be herded into a different area. They'd do that and meanwhile the other cameras were panning over to the next set. So then the audience was shoved over that way and it just looked completely full. It was all very controlled; never a real mess. It was organised chaos.

RUTH

It was a very exciting place then. You became friends with the people you worked with, like the cameramen, the chippies, the lighting men, the vision mixer – they were all very talented people, and all very important.

One brilliant lighting man was Richie Richardson, a lovely man. Ron, he was Camera 1. We got to know everybody very well, and they got to know us. It was very much team work. We were all relatively young, and we were all learning together. Even the ones who were a bit older were enthused by it all.

DEE DEE

Usually we did our own number on *Top of the Pops* and sometimes we also did a backing number. The audience just needed a little bit of encouragement from us to start dancing, otherwise they'd just stand around looking gormless. So it was up to Flick and us to do a bit of clapping and a little bit of movement just to get everybody going. We did quite a few numbers like this with Marc Bolan.

There were accidents, of course. In July 1969 we did a routine for 'Gimme Gimme Good Lovin'', by Crazy Elephant, and Andi's top fell down in the middle. She was a very well-endowed girl and we were wearing small crop-tops with a hanging fringe. When you shimmied, everything moved. And we were shimmying like mad, so much so that Andi parted company with her top. I have never seen anyone move so fast as she dashed off that stage.

Ruthie was the worst one before a show. We'd be doing the countdown and she'd be so nervous that, as they went "30, 29, 28…", she'd say, "Oh my God. What's that step? Is it the right leg or the left leg? Or which one…" We used to say, "Oh shut up, Ruth. Just get on with it."

I was nervous too sometimes. The only ones who were terribly laidback were Babs and Louise. And Flick was pretty easygoing.

RUTH

I used to get very nervous before a show and freak everyone else out. So eventually I was banned from talking to the rest of them about half an hour before the show, and I used to wander round the back of the set by myself to pass the time. In the end I made friends with all the chippies and had cups of tea with them.

BABS

I loved working in television. I liked the intimacy of it. There's one trick that a cameraman in the early days taught me. He said pretend your audience is beyond me, and don't think you're dancing for the camera. You're dancing for that person in the lounge, beyond the camera.

STANLEY APPEL

If you were directing Pan's People you'd be up in the control room and the cameramen would be down on the studio floor, all with their headphones on. And if you got to a sequence where it was unscripted, you'd say casually, "Give us a shot of one of the girls please" – and four cameras would go immediately onto Babs. Everybody loved Babs. I'm not saying they didn't love the other girls, but I think Babs was the favourite amongst the camera crew.

PAUL SMITH

It was the most wonderful time to work in British television. Television was just exploding. We were going into colour, the BBC and ITV were slugging it out, and the audiences were huge. It was just the most fantastic period of time.

DEE DEE

In the summer of 1969 we did another BBC2 series with Bobbie Gentry, then on July the 26th we started rehearsing for *The Frankie Howerd Show* on ITV. The first programme went out on the 9th of August.

Frankie Howerd was very strange. A genius, of course, but a misogynist – he didn't like women at all. We did six shows for him and used to call him "Mr Howerd". There was no "Frankie this" or "Frankie that". If you passed him in the corridors you'd say "Good morning, Mr Howerd." And if he actually replied, you'd think, "Well, at least he answered…"

He didn't get close to us at all. He didn't really like us. We had numbers to do on the show and he also got us to do sketches with him. He'd plant us in the audience and ask for questions, and then we'd have to put our hands up to ask the question.

BABS

We did a series of six shows with Frankie Howerd, shot up at Elstree. The first three, he didn't speak to us at all – unless we were doing some little sketches with him. And it was one morning while doing the fourth show that I just went up to him and said, "Good morning, Mr Howerd!" He looked at me as if he were thinking, where did that come from? And then he rather grudgingly said "Good morning."

That was the only conversation we had in six weeks of working together.

We also did a gig with him at the Café Royal one New Year's Eve, for a charity dinner. We were doing two routines and he was doing his act. I saw him as we came up the stairs to make our entrance. He had his back to us and was facing the wall, preparing. He used to get very nervous. Every "Ooh" and every "Ah" was memorised; he had brilliant timing.

Anyway, he walked out on stage and gave us the most sensational introduction, about this absolutely fantastic group of dancers etc etc – then came off stage and completely blanked us. Then we went out and did our routine. Not a word of conversation.

I think he was very depressed; a very sad man.

RUTH

For *The Frankie Howerd Show* on ITV, Penny Fergusson took my place in Pan's so that I could concentrate on choreographing *Decidedly Dusty* over on BBC1.

Dusty Springfield was fascinating and wonderful. I liked her very much, but she could be difficult. Not with me personally, but sometimes she'd just shut herself in her dressing room. And we'd wait an hour, an hour and a half, two hours, for people to coax her out.

But she was wonderful and taught me a lot. By her own admission she wasn't a great mover, but she quite rightly said that, because she was singing, the breathing is different. She taught me to be aware of what her breathing would be and let that dictate what would be easy for her to move to. It was a big lesson learnt. And I was very proud of that show because I got a good write-up doing that.

Spike Milligan was the special guest in the first show. I remember being a bit awestruck by him, but in rehearsals he was quite quiet. Then, come the actual show, he was waiting to come on while Dusty was singing and he kept popping his head out from the wings. I think they had to stop recording because the audience started laughing. He was an interesting character.

DEE DEE

On the 20th of November we did *The Price of Fame* with Georgie Fame and Alan Price on BBC2. Again, it was with Stanley Dorfman. I think we did four of those, including the Christmas Day special.

Georgie Fame and Alan Price on **The Price of Fame.**

RUTH

One of my abiding memories of *The Price of Fame* was dancing to 'The Clapping Song', which Georgie sang with Billy Preston. Because it goes in a round, we were in three couples; I was partnered with Flick. Anyway, Georgie got the words wrong. So some of us followed the words he was singing, while some of us ignored what he was singing and did the movements as choreographed. It was really really fast and it was utterly hysterical. I have this vision of our manager in the wings pulling his hair out. Flick and I were facing each other and nearly wetting ourselves laughing. It was an utter mess.

DEE DEE

On the 14th of December we were up in Leeds doing a 60-minute special for Yorkshire Television called *George Martin Presents – With a Little Help from My Friends*, which was directed by a young director called David Mallett and went out on Christmas Eve. It was a big A-list show featuring Ringo Starr, Spike Milligan, Dudley Moore, Lulu, Blue Mink, The Hollies, and us.

Ruthie and I backed Ringo on the song 'Octopus's Garden'. We were stuck in the bowels of the earth with him in a yellow submarine which rose up through the studio floor. It juddered all the way up, but I wasn't complaining. Who would, being stuck with a real-live Beatle?

The wonderful thing about that particular show was the guests on it. When we were finished we all jumped onto the train back to London. Not in first class – I think it was just standard class. So there, in the middle of this train, were sitting Pan's People and Dudley Moore. I don't know what the rest of the passengers must have thought. It was just before Christmas and we were all in very high spirits. Dudley was adorable. All he did the whole time was tell us stories and crack jokes.

It was such a wonderful, wonderful moment.

FIVE
CATWALKS AND
PRAT FALLS
1970

★★★★★★★★★★★★★★★★★★★★★★★★★★★★★★★★★★★★★

DEE DEE

In January 1970 there was a picture of us in the *Evening Standard* saying that we'd signed a 'contract' agreeing not to get married for two years. It was a bit of publicity for a number we were doing on *Top of the Pops* that week called 'Wedding Bell Blues' by The 5th Dimension. We were all dressed in mini wedding dresses and veils. As it turned out, Andi went ahead and got married just before our time was up, in December 1971.

We'd been doing *Top of the Pops* for a year at TV Centre. But now Stanley Dorfman changed the format and made it a 45-minute show, which meant expanding it from the Top 20 to the Top 30. Stanley and an up-and-coming director called Mel Cornish took it in turns to direct. And it very much changed the feel of the show; some bands did a couple of numbers, and more album groups had a chance to appear.

There was a particularly memorable *Top of the Pops* moment on February the 25th. We were in Studio 8 when John Lennon and Yoko Ono appeared on the show, performing 'Instant Karma'. They were sporting short-cropped hair and were dressed in denim unisex baggy suits. Yoko had a sort of blindfold on her head that looked like a sanitary towel. Not only that, but she was knitting at the same time.

★ ★ ★ ★ ★ ★

OPPOSITE:
Andi, Dee Dee, Babs and Louise record a routine for **Top of the Pops** *– Flick and Ruth are to the right of Louise but out of frame.*

The wedding photo – in costume to perform 'Wedding Bell Blues' on **Top of the Pops.**

RUTH

On *Top of the Pops* we were all trying to make the best programme we could and experimenting with new television techniques. Flick worked out all the camera scripts, which hadn't really been done before for dancing. In the past, dancers would do a routine and the director would just tell the cameras which shot he wanted. But our routines were choreographed especially for that shot. Sometimes we would just dance a bit that was for the camera and then cut to three other girls dancing. Then when we weren't on camera, we were running around to get into position for another camera shot. It was quite innovative for the time.

DEE DEE

Our dance contemporaries were The Irving Davies Dancers, a group called The Love Machine who did the odd thing here and there, and The Young Generation.

There must have been between 20 or 30 dancers in The Young Generation. There was no sort of individuality about them; they were just all part of an enormous group run by Stuart Morris, who was head of Light Entertainment. One of the members of The Young Generation was a young, very talented dancer called Nigel Lythgoe.

The thing that was unique about Pan's People was that we were a group in our own right, like a pop group. We never swapped dancers, so everybody knew each one of us and who we were.

SUE

What Flick was doing had never been done before. The Young Generation, for example, was a mass of 20-odd dancers, but you couldn't pick out one over any other. Flick, however, would use each girl for her looks and ability and work on that basis.

STANLEY APPEL

The stage on *Top of the Pops* was over three feet high; you couldn't let the dancers dance on the floor, or else you couldn't get your low-angle shots.

If you've got a girl with a lovely pair of legs, the best way to show them is from a low angle because, if you crane up and shoot her from a high angle, she's got tiny little legs. So, photographically, a dancer looks better if she's shot from lower down.

Also, when the audience came in, the dancers had to be higher than the floor or else you'd never see them among the audience. Around the set was a tiny little sort of trip thing so the girls would know when they got to the end of the stage. Fortunately, I can't recall anybody falling off.

BABS

There was one time when Ruth and I were doing a little duet and suddenly it became a solo. Ruth just disappeared off the back of the stage. You knew that if you made a mistake there was nothing you could do about it. If you made a mistake and missed a step then everybody saw it.

SUE

Flick used to say, "If you make a mistake, just keep dancing." We never used to re-take our routines; you literally had to fall over. And we made some mistakes that still went out. It was a case of trying not to go wrong, really. And if you did, just keep moving. No one will notice!

BABS

Whatever happened, you carried on. If you were ill you went to the doctor, got a Vitamin B jab and did the show. If somebody did have to be off for whatever reason, we covered. The show always went on.

I remember one time when I had a really bad abscess on my tooth. My face looked like a chipmunk, it was so swollen. So the night before I managed to see a dentist, who extracted the tooth and put me on painkillers.

DEE DEE

We used to sometimes do fashion shows, one of which was staged at the Royal Garden Hotel in Kensington for a company called Pippa Dee Parties. We were all wearing these cute little numbers. But the problem was that the hotel wouldn't let us have a rehearsal. So, of course, it turned into a complete farce.

It was just a scream, because the compere would be saying "Here comes Dee Dee in some beautiful lingerie" and there'd be an empty stage – there'd be nobody coming out at all. And in the background you could hear people saying, "Quick, quick. Where's my bra? Where's my top?"

So there were these huge gaps in the show while we were struggling into our costumes. The whole thing was a complete and utter disaster.

BABS

Ruth was supposed to do a bit of dancing at the end of the catwalk, and

then I had to come out, run gently down the catwalk and do a little leapfrog over Ruth.

When I came to put on my costume, Ruth had already gone. And to my horror, as I put on my slip, I realised that it would be very hard to do the leapfrog wearing this little slip. So I thought, "I know what I'll do. I'll just run down as I'm supposed to, and at the last minute I'll hitch the slip up to my waist, put my hands down and do my leapfrog."

Ruth, as she was doing a little spin, saw me make my entrance, spotted

Costumes inspired by **The Forsyte Saga** *for The* **Carpenters'** *'(They Long to Be) Close to You' on* **Top of the Pops,** *15 October 1970.*

the slip and thought, "Oh my God. Babs will never get over me wearing that. I've got to duck so she can do her jump." But I was looking up at the audience and didn't see Ruth duck down. I hitched up my slip, put my hands down for Ruth and there was nothing there. There was only air.

All they heard backstage was a loud thud as I hit the deck. And then I slid forward – because it was quite shiny – like an aeroplane coming in to land. I slid forward to the end of the runway and managed to stop just before the end. Then I looked up, straight into the face of our sponsor.

I managed to get up and stagger off stage. I quickly changed into my final costume and we all went out again. And then I heard a gasp from some of the ladies in the audience and thought, "Gosh, what's happened?" I looked down and realised I'd grazed my arms from the wrist to the elbow; blood was dripping onto my costume.

So it was a fairly disastrous occasion. Needless to say, we weren't invited back.

DEE DEE

On the 23rd of April 1970 we went off to Brize Norton to film with the Royal Marines, along with Jimmy Savile. I remember doing the assault course. We climbed up one side of a wooden structure, walked along it, went to the end, and there were two gorgeous young Marines waiting to catch us. And guess what? When I jumped down, they dropped me. My eyelash went flying off, and there I was with just one. I wasn't especially pleased about that – I had a sore eye for the rest of the day.

BABS

They put us through the assault course. I remember crawling underneath the nets and trying to scramble over the rope fences. And Dee Dee was sitting astride the bikers, the pyramid that they make with motorbikes.

RUTH

I found it very difficult, and very cold. The best bit was being invited to dinner afterwards. We finished filming, got changed and were in the lobby when one of the soldiers came back from training and almost fainted on the floor. Nothing to do with us! He was just so exhausted. I really take my hat off to them. Their training is so tough, absolutely brutal.

DEE DEE

Towards the end of the day we were having a break and standing by the main gates when suddenly there was an enormous kerfuffle outside. Some young lad had been cycling past and had spotted Pan's People standing there. He was so surprised that he came a cropper and fell off his bike, and was knocked unconscious. When he opened his eyes, he had Jimmy Savile and Pan's People all leaning over him, administering first aid.

BABS

We'd change in the back of Jimmy's van. He had this Winnebago-type van that had beds and a kitchenette in it, which he'd travel all over the country in. I remember thinking at the time that it made perfect sense to have something like that, because you can't always be reliant on hotels. And he did so much travelling. But we had no idea about the dreadful goings-on that subsequently came to light.

DEE DEE

Our paths crossed with Jimmy Savile constantly because of *Top of the Pops*. I hated him. I used to see young girls lining up outside his van and knew there was something wrong there. If a young dancer who's not the brightest button on the beach, who's preoccupied with her dancing, her make-up and her hair could notice that, and notice how slimy and repulsive he was, then surely other people noticed too.

I thought he was the most hypocritical little creep; the only person he was interested in was himself. As long as the limelight was on him. He'd come up to you to say hello but, if he suddenly saw a camera over your shoulder, he'd just keep walking. If he stopped, he'd always kiss your hand… but he'd almost lick it. He was just revolting.

CHERRY

I was only 17 when I joined Pan's in 1972. I cannot express how naïve I was at that point in my life. And when I first appeared on the set, Jimmy Savile came over to introduce himself and French-kissed my hand, which I found one of the most repulsive acts ever.

From that day on, whenever I knew he was around or was on the show, I would make myself very scarce. You just have an instinct. He never did anything to me. You just didn't want to be in his vicinity. Unfortunately, because we were all BBC artists, there were lots of things we had to do with Jimmy.

DEE DEE

We felt very uncomfortable about Jimmy but were more or less bulldozed into being nice to him. He was extremely popular and powerful at the Beeb. So when he said to me "You must come and see my van," I almost felt obliged to. I asked Louise to come with me because I was too uncomfortable to go into his minibus on my own.

I remember walking up the steps and there he was, sitting in the driving seat and smoking a cigar. He leered at us and said, "Have a look in there."

I opened the door and there was this enormous bed. Nothing else, just a seven-foot bed in the back compartment. "This is his knocking shop," I remember thinking distinctly. "Oh my God, how repulsive." Shutting the door and feeling terribly uncomfortable, we made our excuses and quickly left. But he really wasn't interested in us; he was interested in much younger girls.

And a lot of the girls who used to come onto *Top of the Pops* were very young. I think at some point there was a rule made that they had to be 16 and over. But they didn't take their passports with them, and a lot of the young girls looked older anyway. Jimmy used to make a bee-line for them. He was always surrounded by pretty young girls. And he was just creepy.

At that time, we were all young girls in our mid-twenties and he was about 45. He was a creepy old guy to us, so you can imagine how he seemed to the younger girls. But he was an iconic figure. What young girl wasn't going to accept a lift in Jimmy's gold Rolls-Royce?

BABS

We thought that what Jimmy did for charity, what he did with the hospitals, was down to earth and very admirable. We hadn't a clue about what was actually occurring. Broadmoor was one of his causes, so, a few years after the filming at Brize Norton, we were asked to go there to do a show. Jimmy went out on stage in one of the halls and introduced us. And we went out and did a few dance routines. And then we were taken to meet the governor and some of the patients.

CHERRY

Performing at Broadmoor? What a ridiculous idea! Whose brain thought that up? To have Pan's People perform for all those prisoners… They had some kind of theatre set-up there, and we did our routines on stage. We were followed everywhere by armed guards, but even scarier was the fact that Jimmy had the keys to every single door in that place.

SIX
MALTA AND
MOMBASA
1971

★★★★★★★★★★★★★★★★★★★★★★★★★★★★★★★★

DEE DEE

It was in 1971 that we parted company with Jim Ramble and began to manage ourselves. Which was probably not a very nice thing to do, because we owed so much to James. If not for James coming along and looking after us and getting us work, we might never have got *Top of the Pops*.

OPPOSITE & ABOVE:
On the HMS London in Valletta harbour, May 1971.

Anyway, early that year we did yet another BBC2 series with Bobbie Gentry, then in May we were invited by the Royal Navy to Malta to dance on the HMS London. The BBC filmed it. We danced to 'Walking' by CCS. I've got a picture of us all leaning over the railings in our little smocks. I think we had frilly knickers on, which must have pleased the sailors.

Flick and Dee Dee enjoy a drink with Royal Navy sailors.

STANLEY APPEL

When Pan's were asked to go to Malta to entertain the forces, I spoke to Flick and she said, "Yeah, that would be OK. We'll be able to fit it in with our schedules." Naturally I had to fit it in with the head of the department too, and also asked if I could bring a film crew along. So that's what we did. We took a small crew and during the time the girls were free, having done their performance, we shot a film. It was a very enjoyable time.

BABS

The fleet massed in Valletta harbour for three days of shows. The BBC film crew stayed on board HMS Eagle and we stayed in the Wrenery. We were very cross because we wanted to stay on board ship, but women weren't allowed in those days.

RUTH

I think, in retrospect, it was probably wise we didn't stay on board.

We were piped aboard HMS Eagle. We shouldn't have been, as only the Queen is supposed to be piped on board. So it was quite an honour. I remember the Admiral invited us onto his frigate for dinner. We were all in evening dresses and mine was cut quite low. As we boarded the ship the Admiral wasn't looking me in the eye at all.

BRYAN SHOWELL
BBC SOUND ASSISTANT

I was booked to film a *Top of the Pops* item involving Pan's People, Combined Services Entertainment and the Royal Navy in Malta. The whole roadshow, technicians and artists, travelled together in a coach and by air.

The shoot took place over a weekend – we went out Friday and came back Monday – and in that time we filmed a dance routine with the girls and shot some of the Combined Services show for the troops, with artists including Johnny Ball and Janet Brown. We had a great time that weekend. On the Sunday night I managed to have a few too many drinks, along with some of the *Top of the Pops* production crew and a few sailors.

When not filming or rehearsing for the show, the girls were being looked after royally by the Navy. They were very popular with the sailors.

DEE DEE

I became the ship's mascot. There used to be an advertisement for Double Diamond beer that ran: "A Double Diamond works wonders, works wonders…" And the sailors used to sing to me, "A Double Dee Dee works wonders, works wonders."

RUTH

We did seem to have a connection with all the forces. I'm sure they did more for our egos than we ever did for them. They used to give us special guided tours, even into the boiler rooms. It was wonderful.

BABS

Lads from all the different ships were doing their rehearsals on board their own ships. I remember joking with one of the officers; he said that if the Russians got hold of some of the information that was circulating between the ships, about the things that they were doing, they would wonder what on earth was going on.

BRYAN SHOWELL

Anchored at Valletta harbour was not only HMS Eagle but also HMS Glasgow and HMS Glamorgan, and a few frigates as well. There were also a number of Russian ships observing our fleet: this was still Cold War time. Sometimes the frigates would have a 'steam up' to confuse our Russian friends, involving the ship moving out of the harbour into the Med, then turning back to Valletta and dropping anchor.

DEE DEE

Right at the end, we went up to the highest cliff in Malta and the whole of the fleet left the harbour. And as they left the harbour, they did a salute to everyone watching. All the ships blew their horns. It just made me feel so nostalgic and so British. We had the most amazing time, it was just fantastic.

BABS

Watching from the ramparts of Valletta harbour when the fleet left was probably one of the most moving things I've ever seen – all the lads in their uniforms and the bands playing. I had tears streaming down my face.

DEE DEE

As well as Flick choreographing us, we also had Tessa Watts-Russell, who

Dancing on the deck of HMS London to 'Walking' by CCS.

joined us quite early on as our choreologist. She basically wrote down all the dances Flick devised so they could be remembered. She was lovely, Tessa. She came with us everywhere.

TESSA WATTS-RUSSELL

I was in my final year at college, the Institute of Choreology in London, and I thought that I'd like to work in television. I wrote to all the choreographers who were involved in light entertainment at the time, and Flick Colby responded. Flick was very interested in dance notation and what it meant and it just went from there.

Choreology is the notation of movement; it's just a way of recording dance routines, because film alone wasn't necessarily good enough to learn back a routine. As it turned out, I didn't really have time to make full master scores of all their work, because no sooner had they finished one routine than they were on to the next.

They very proudly used to introduce me as their choreologist, but I was also their PA and – I don't think they'll mind if I say so – general dogsbody. If there was a job that needed doing, I got on and did it. Very soon I was answering all their fan mail, liaising with directors and producers, and going out on location with them when they went filming.

I was with them for four years. As it turned out, there wasn't much of a call for me to teach back their routines. But it was an amazing first job to have, absolutely extraordinary.

DEE DEE

We did everything to the words as well as the music. If it was "I love you," you'd point to yourself and then you'd point to someone else and put your hand on your heart.

SUE

Pan's People were always being accused of the old hand mime. But that changed. And then, as disco came in, you didn't have the time for gestures – dance would be more about the feet. And so that went out the window. It was a style Flick used, just something that she did for a while. A bit like fashion; one day you're wearing flares and the next you're in drainpipes.

BABS

Flick went through different styles. There were certainly a few routines that I'd rather not remember, and unfortunately those are the ones that tend to be remembered by others! 'The Monster Mash', in September 1973, was one. I was a kind of Martian, painted green and in a silver costume with bug eyes coming through a funny head-dress. Ruth was King Kong, Dee Dee was a mummy with a rose between her teeth, Louise a vampire in top hat and tails, and Cherry a cute little bat. Noel Edmonds called us 'Fangs People'. That's one that I'd like to go to the graveyard of dance routines!

DEE DEE

In July 1971 we nipped over to Brussels to compete once again in the Golden Sea Swallow of Knokke competition. Stanley Dorfman came over to direct it, with a new young star called Lance LeGault, who had been in a West End musical Flick had choreographed called *Catch My Soul*. He was tall and beautiful and blond, and sang wonderfully. Flick choreographed and we won Best Show. So that was quite nice, especially for Stanley, who'd worked so hard on it. Lance LeGault went back to America, and played lots of colonels. He was in *The A-Team* eventually.

Then on the 10th of December Andi got married to a chap called Gerald Mendes da Costa at Finchley Road register office. Straight after that we flew to Mombasa to entertain the Navy – us and the entertainment corps, ENSA. We flew over in a Hercules and of course Babs tried to fly the plane again.

Our director Vernon Lawrence came too, with his BBC crew. They made a sort of roughshod stage for us on the aircraft carrier HMS Triumph, and the audience all sat where the planes came in and watched us doing our dance. We did a number called 'Montego Bay' where we had these suits which we stripped off to reveal bikinis. And then we spent about two or three days filming there. It was so hot and we were getting sunburnt and all that, but it was great fun.

BABS

The BBC came out with us and filmed the show, and also filmed us on the beaches and around the town. We were only supposed to be there for three days.

RUTH

For the return flight we all got onto the RAF Hercules plane again, and I was sitting opposite the crew when they sat down for take-off. And it was very strange because there was absolute silence. I was watching their faces and you could tell instinctively that something wasn't right.

BABS

I was sitting with Johnny Ball and he was telling me naughty stories as we were about to take off. We were sitting behind the radio engineer and, as we built up speed for take-off, I heard, over his cans, the captain saying, "We're going to have to stop. Put the plane into emergency reverse thrust. Now! Now! Go!" And then the plane made a screeching noise. I remember getting off the plane quite calmly and seeing Andi in hysterics.

RUTH

We all ran straight to the bar. The pilot was already there, white, with all the crew, drinking a large whisky. And we then found out that everybody watching had been horrified. Because when the plane went into reverse, the tyres caught on fire. There was a precipice at the end of the runway and we'd only stopped just in time, apparently.

BABS

We were then told that if we'd been in a civil airline they would've had to take off and the plane would've plunged into the ravine. I think there's a point between 90 and 120 miles an hour in which the plane has the opportunity to stop, and we had gone beyond it. But because it was an RAF plane, because it was military, the brilliant captain managed to stop. And that saved our lives.

DEE DEE

We all trooped back to the Mombasa Nyali beach hotel where we'd been staying, which was absolutely lovely. And we actually spent another three or four days in Mombasa because we couldn't get back to England – all the planes were grounded in the heat. So we missed the Christmas *Top of*

Performing to 'Another Day' by Paul McCartney on **Top of the Pops,** *11 March 1971.*

the Pops. They had to rehash some old numbers of ours and just put them together and put that on the show, because we weren't there.

BABS

Our parents received a telegram to say that we were involved in this difficult situation regarding planes. They didn't know how or when we would be getting back. There was this big debate going on between the BBC, the government and the Navy about who was actually going to fly us back. Eventually it was the Navy that forked out and flew us all back on a civil airliner.

DEE DEE

So we went all the way to Nairobi to get a commercial plane back to

England, which was great because there was nobody on this particular plane; there were only about 20 people. So we had all these seats and spare room and sort of stretched out and had a good old sleep, because in the past week we'd hardly slept at all.

BABS

While I was away my parents received another dreadful telegram, saying that my brother had gone missing in Nigeria. They debated about whether to tell me while I was out in Mombasa. And it's probably a good job they didn't. Because otherwise I would have said, "Girls, I'm going to Nigeria."

DEE DEE

Babs' parents were at the airport to meet her – and that's when they told her. But they didn't tell us, which was very kind of them. I felt they didn't want to upset us. A couple of days later, the phone rang in my flat; it was Tessa Watts-Russell calling.

She said, "Dee Dee, have you heard about John?"

I said, "No. I haven't heard from him lately, but I'm expecting a letter."

She said, "He's gone missing."

I was so shocked. John had been my boyfriend for quite a few years. We were very close. It was really horrible, because he was such a lovely boy.

Babs' brother John Lord.

BABS

John had become a professional deep-sea diver and had joined an Italian oil company; he'd been with them for a year or so.

His work involved off-shore diving from a ship, and he was on his way to his ship when the outboard motor of his RIB packed in. Apparently John was with a younger and less experienced diver, and it was decided that as he was the senior and stronger of the two he would try and swim the half mile to the ship, in dangerous waters.

Tragically, he didn't make it. My brother, and only sibling, never came home.

SEVEN
FAME
1972

★★

DEE DEE

1972 was the year of Gary Glitter, The Sweet, David Bowie, Wizzard and
Mott the Hoople. Every band suddenly decided that they wanted to wear
the glitziest outfits possible.

I felt very sorry for the BBC make-up department. Every week on *Top
of the Pops*, there were more men in the make-up room than there were
girls. All putting their lipstick on and having their hair done. There was so
much glitter. Glittering all-in-one costumes; hot pants in glitter;
everything in glitter. We had an awful lot to compete with.

ED STEWART
PRESENTER, TOP OF THE POPS

I first met Pan's People when I did the programme on 30 December
1971. And what a lovely bunch of girls they were.

I had a patch over my eye because I'd grazed my eyeball with my
contact lens the day before and had been advised by my doctor to wear an
eye-patch, to avoid infection.

"But I'm doing *Top of the Pops* tomorrow," I pointed out.

"Well," he replied, "you'll look different, won't you?"

The Pan's girls joined me for the show links. Babs happened to kiss me
during the first one, so after that I insisted the rest of them did too. Well,
when you're surrounded by beautiful women you've got to make the most
of it!

OPPOSITE:
*Soon to give up
dancing, Flick
(right) poses with
Louise, Babs, Ruth,
Dee and Andi for a
publicity photo by
Frazer Wood.*

DEE DEE

In April Flick gave up dancing with the group because her commitments on the choreography side were taking precedence. It had got to the point where we were doing so much that poor Flick found it very difficult to both choreograph and be in the numbers. Sometimes we might do a show where we did a lot of dancing and she'd be a beat behind or would do something wrong. Not through her own fault, but because she couldn't rehearse as much as we could. It just became too much for her.

RUTH

In a way, it was much better, because it was too much for Flick. Plus, I don't think she enjoyed performing that much. We became a tighter unit. There was just a different dynamic, but it worked. Because she could concentrate on the choreography and the whole concept, she had more control over designing our costumes, designing the set and so on. She had time to script and experiment more with the technical side of things. So I'd say we all benefited from that. She was a great dancer, but I think we became much more professional after she left.

PAUL SMITH

Flick would come up to the gallery whenever the dance routines were being taped. I think she even ended up sitting in the director's seat. Some of the directors would get up and let her actually direct it, because she'd choreographed it and had decided where the shots should be taken from. She became very skilled in doing that.

STANLEY DORFMAN

For the first couple of years I'd go to the outside rehearsal and we'd script it from Flick's rough dance. But as the years went on she became more and more involved and would in fact choreograph the moves to specific cameras; we had four of five cameras at the time. So it made my job really easy, and made me look very good when it was really all her doing! And

then when she stopped dancing to concentrate on the choreography, I'd just let her sit down and direct the whole thing.

With **Top of the Pops** *director* ***Vernon Lawrence*** *and (bottom right) musical director* ***Johnny Pearson.***

DEE DEE

Flick knew what she wanted, and choreography-wise there was only one chief. We used to complain sometimes, because she made us do things that were terribly difficult. But you can't have a whole lot of chiefs; you do have to have the Indians. Basically, we were the Indians and she was the chief.

BABS

Flick was our mother, really; we deferred to her in everything. We valued

One of Flick's last performances with the group, Top of the Pops, 24 February 1972.

her opinions and trusted her implicitly, even when we did some pretty dire things. Her ideas towards the latter days of Pan's People got a little quirky and avant-garde. But even so, she was the skipper of the ship. There could only be one skipper and Flick was it.

RUTH

Flick was the one in charge. Although we liked to think of ourselves as a democracy, she had more say than most. When we went away we quite often shared hotel rooms together. We just got on very well. And obviously, because we worked together for much longer, managing Legs & Co and Ruby Flipper, we knew each other extremely well. We went through a lot together.

★ ★ ★ ★ ★

DEE DEE

In May of 1972, we did a big slimming campaign. One very hot day, we filmed in some long grass right on the river for a BBC programme called *Nationwide*, presented by Frank Bough. And then they had us on the programme, promoting our slimming campaign. We were interviewed for newspaper articles saying what we ate and didn't eat, and that exercise was very good for you. Even if we didn't always follow our own advice!

That year we were doing loads of gigs in different places. We opened a men's shop in Rochford called Grand Detours. We did an enormous promotion for Multi-Glide car oil. And then we did a gig in Glasgow for Tiffanys. So it was very much a year where we were flitting here, there and everywhere.

RUTH

Sometimes we were hired to go and open a clothes shop or something like that. We spent two-thirds of the week shut up in a cold, dirty rehearsal room, plus one day in the studio and then a few days travelling all over the country doing gigs.

DEE DEE

On May the 25th we did a big gig in Newcastle for a new boutique called Victoria and Albert.

Our driver, Ken, drove us up in our black Daimler limousine. But when we got to the venue, there were hundreds and hundreds of people blocking the entrance to the street. It was quite frightening, as the fans were pressing on the windows and banging on the car, shouting our names. There was an enormous cordon of police there, linking arms, trying to keep the crowds at bay. It was really scary.

So poor Ken had to back up the car and drive around the block, by which time the police had managed to control the crowd a bit more. So we were able to finally get out and go into the shop.

But it was an alarming experience, because with all the pressure on the car windows we were worried they'd collapse in on us. People were queuing up for hours and hours. I signed over 600 autographs that day.

Anyway, around this time Andi told us she was pregnant. We were really shocked and upset; it didn't come at a very good time. We felt that we were really just beginning to make it then, so we didn't want Andi to go.

RUTH

We knew that her leaving would be problematical. But not just that – we were an incredibly close-knit family. We were like sisters.

DEE DEE

In September Andi went off to have her baby girl. So we decided that we needed another girl in the group to do the cabaret gigs until she came back.

CHERRY

I can't ever remember not dancing. It was just something I could do as soon as I could walk. I loved music, and felt as though the music was somehow inside me. We had a lot of music at home thanks to my father, who was a musician and had his own band. He had his serious job and then would reappear at 6.00 pm in evening dress to go off and play at some dinner dance or other. And my mother sang to my sister and me all the time – we were always singing.

So it was really the most natural thing for me to be at tap and ballet class, aged five. The training escalated as I got older, and I was entered into the All England Sunshine dancing competitions. At one event the judges took my parents to one side and suggested that they take my training to another level. Everything pointed to the Bush Davies School in East Grinstead, but it was a huge decision for my parents. We were such a happy unit, so for me to go away to school was a big wrench. However, I'd read all the Enid Blyton Mallory Towers books, and boarding school turned out to be just as much fun!

School was hard work. We were up at the crack of dawn, started school work at 9.00 am and then from three o'clock we started all our dance classes. It all ended around 9.00 pm, when you fell into bed. You just ran from one class to another class to another class. Physically, it's very difficult as well. But when you're that age and you love what you're doing, that's what you do. It gives you fantastic discipline. I'm frighteningly self-disciplined still, and I'm sure that's why.

Looking back, some of our teachers were incredibly eccentric. Miss Bush – hence the name of the school – was 'she who must be obeyed'. She entered a room and everyone curtsied. The respect was extraordinary. In her classes nobody spoke, nobody did anything they weren't meant to do. She'd come up to you and physically 'right' you into place. But I think every single girl would say they feel grateful for the training we got. There was a lot of shouting and screaming and throwing things, but none of us seemed to suffer very much. It seemed to do the trick.

We were very occasionally allowed to watch television. So of course I'd seen Pan's People, but that certainly wasn't the career path I envisaged. Miss Bush wanted me to be a ballerina because – although I went to Bush Davies to be a jazz dancer and, primarily, an actress – I was doing incredibly well in ballet as well. My last year I danced the role of Swanhilda in *Coppelia* and got wonderful reviews in the *Telegraph*. So at that point, I was a little confused as to what I was going to do, and was being pulled in all sorts of directions.

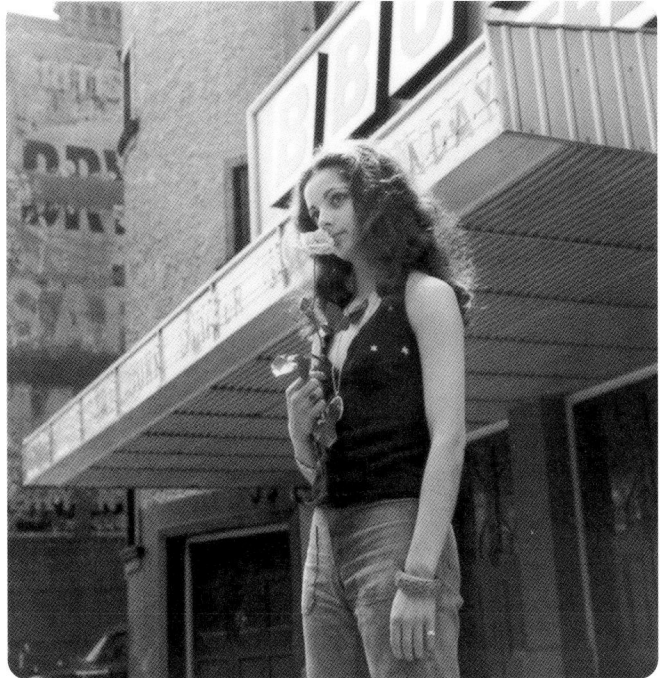

Cherry at the BBC Television Theatre in Shepherd's Bush early in 1973.

In those days, to progress you had to have your Equity card, come what may. And to get this Equity card, you had to first of all have a provisional card, which you could get by performing in a regional theatre. We were very lucky at Bush Davies, because we had a theatre that had been built in the grounds called the Adeline Genée Theatre. And during school holidays this theatre went professional; there was a rep company in there. So I stayed over the holidays sometimes, appearing in professional productions in order to get my provisional Equity card.

I auditioned for the Royal Festival Ballet. It came down to two of us, and it was me at 5'2" and the other girl at 5'7". There was a sort of fashion at the time to have very tall ballerinas, and the tall girl got the place instead of me. I was devastated.

Anyway, within days I was living in London, having left Bush Davies in September, and had an agent. And my agent said to me, "The best thing you can do now is go to every single audition you read about in *The Stage* and just get some experience. Just do everything."

And, unbelievably, the very first audition I went to was for Pan's People.

They were looking for a girl to do their cabaret performances because Andrea Rutherford was pregnant. Although she could get away with still being on *Top of the Pops*, what she didn't want to do was rush around the country doing all the gigs they used to do. So they needed somebody just to step in and do the cabaret. And I thought that would get me my full Equity card.

The audition was at the Dance Centre, right at the very top of the building. There were so many girls there. The queue wound round the building and up the stairs and I just waited and thought, "Oh, good grief."

DEE DEE

We held an audition at the Dance Centre, the place that we'd left a few years before – in the room right at the top. And the four of us sat there, a little bit like the Gestapo, and all these women filed past us.

RUTH

We were just gobsmacked. There must have been thousands of girls, because the building was very large and they were queuing outside. We couldn't believe it.

I remember seeing Cherry and just saying, "That's the one." I think we all did. She was pretty, she was a brilliant dancer, she had personality. She had everything we were looking for.

DEE DEE

I remember this little thing coming up the stairs with long curly hair and, the moment she came around the corner, I thought, "That's the one." She had this angelic little face and this long hair and this very petite, pretty figure. She was very elfin-looking. But a beautiful dancer. And that was Cherry Gillespie. We all decided she was the one we wanted. So she joined us.

CHERRY

They chose me. To this day I have no idea why. I really don't. Nobody was more surprised than me and my agent. I'd been in London for about two days.

I think the intention was that Andrea was going to come back. I was only required to do those weeks when she was pregnant and having the baby. But, as time went on, it became more and more obvious that Andrea wasn't going to be back.

DEE DEE

Andi had a baby, which she called Louise, after our Louise; they were great friends. After Pan's she went to Australia with her husband Gerry and the baby.

To begin with, Cherry joined us temporarily for our cabaret shows and just watched us work for the experience. She was very, very young.

At this particular time, we were rehearsing in a place called the Old Oak Club, which was a working men's club in Old Oak Common Lane. It

Cherry (second from right) joins Louise, Babs, Dee Dee and Ruth for rehearsals at the Old Oak Club.

was very convenient, but particularly dreadful, dark and smelled of beer. They loved having Pan's there.

CHERRY

When I got the job, the first thing I had to do was meet them all at a working men's club in Old Oak Common Lane. The BBC had the most dreadful rehearsal spaces, in the weirdest places. So I went to Old Oak Common Lane and they were rehearsing 'The Jean Genie'. I loved that Bowie track so much. I can see myself standing there, watching them rehearse and offering to make them all a cup of tea.

Then it kind of dawned on me… "Oh my God. This is real. This is really going to happen."

They said that I'd better have a look at what they did at TV Centre. I went to the BBC on one of the Wednesdays when they were recording,

The original *Top of the Pops* line-up: Ruth, Andi, Louise, Flick, Dee Dee and Babs, 1968.

ABOVE:
Babs during filming at
Liphook in July 1969.

RIGHT & OPPOSITE:
Babs, Flick, Andi, Louise,
Dee Dee and Ruth back
Marc Bolan on *Top of
the Pops* in the early
1970s.

RIGHT: Babs goes disco.

FAR RIGHT: Louise and Dee Dee in symmetric costumes.

BELOW: 'Dance with the Devil' by Cozy Powell, *Top of the Pops*, December 1973.

LEFT:
Top of the Pops,
January 1974.

BELOW:
The John Denver Show,
May 1973.

RIGHT: Performing with the star of *The John Denver Show*, May 1973.

BELOW: 'Summertime City' with Mike Batt, *Top of the Pops*, 4 September 1975.

OPPOSITE TOP: The infamous shredded jeans appeared in 1975.

OPPOSITE BELOW: At the barre with Eric and Ernie on *The Morecambe and Wise Christmas Show*, December 1975.

Cherry, Dee Dee and Lee perform Elton John's 'Island Girl' on *Top of the Pops*, 16 October 1975.

and that was even more mind-blowing. We were all in the make-up room together, and they were showing me things and introducing me to the girls, when Cliff Richard walked in. I couldn't speak. From five years old I'd watched Cliff Richard. He was such a big star.

Then somebody popped their head in and said, "Girls, can you come onto the set please?" So I was left alone with Cliff Richard in the make-up room. He was so kind and so charming, and so welcoming and sweet, I can't begin to tell you. And from that day, every time he came on the show, he came to find me to see how I was getting on. It was extraordinary.

So then I had to learn all the routines they were doing in cabaret. And have costumes fitted and all that sort of thing. I suddenly realised that there was this whole other world beyond just seeing the girls on television every week.

But while I embarked on the cabaret scene with the girls, unbelievably, I got a letter from the Royal Festival Ballet Company. "Great news, Cherry. A place has become free in the Festival Ballet, and we would very much like you to join the company."

It was so extraordinary that in just two weeks my life had taken a completely different path. I'd already signed my contract with the girls by then and that was it. Done.

And then I kept getting letters from my principal Miss Bush, from Bush Davies, saying how disappointed she was in me. "You're betraying your art and your talent," that sort of thing.

But once I was out of the boarding school situation, I'm not sure that I could have spent five years being on the end of a line in the Festival Ballet, waiting to become a soloist. I'm not sure whether that really would've suited me, looking back. So fate really played a hand in my life, making those decisions for me.

To begin with, I wouldn't see the other girls every day; it would just be whenever we were doing cabaret gigs. I would literally just get a phone call to say, "This is the diary. Can you meet us at such and such?" Or, if we were in the car, "You'll be picked up."

Sometimes we travelled by train, if the gig was in Scotland or somewhere. But if it was at all doable in a car, our chauffeur Ken, who was a lovely man, would drive us in an old Daimler limo. It was big enough for all of us to get in, with the costumes in the back. Then we'd just bomb around, stopping at transport cafés on motorways at God knows what time of night. And people would do a double-take. "No, it can't be…"

Some of the gigs were very small, where wealthy people had paid a lot of money for us to perform at their private birthday parties. Or else there'd be big clubs wanting to open with Pan's People appearing. They weren't long sets, and we talked to the audience and all that sort of thing.

RUTH

Most of our work was done in discos, which was very difficult. They either had a tiny little stage – where maybe a three-piece band might play, or a disc jockey would do his stuff – or we'd have to dance on the dance floor. There might be pillars in between, and there wouldn't be any lighting. No facilities at all. It was very amateurish.

As the years went by, it improved. Once we'd learnt the ropes we'd take our own sound system and ask for at least the minimum amount of lighting. But it wasn't always possible. And we did perform in some of the most ridiculous situations.

SUE

We would do cabaret for conventions or big dinners, where maybe Shell would have their annual dinner at the Grosvenor House Hotel and there would be a cabaret. So we'd be slotted in with someone like a comedian. Every audience was different.

We had a whole cabaret set that we'd do, which Flick would update every so often. Some of it was using singles and some of it was using classic tracks off albums. It could be anything Flick wanted to do, really. I can't remember all the numbers, but we did 'Baby Love' by The Supremes,

Stealers Wheel's 'Stuck in the Middle with You', and 'Move on Up' by Curtis Mayfield. We would go out, do a number and then come back in again. Then 20 minutes later we'd go out and do another number, and so on.

We'd also do gigs at universities. We were very popular with students, though they probably would have been equally pleased to have had a band there. But students really did enjoy the shows. It was a bit of glamour; we'd sign autographs, give out pictures and what have you. Very enthusiastic audiences, one way or another. I think it was probably because they'd all been in the Student Union earlier, downing the pints.

CHERRY

It could get quite out of hand. I remember things got quite wild at Glasgow University. There was huge security, and the security people came to see us backstage and said "Girls, we're a little bit concerned. Don't change. Just grab your stuff and let's get you on the coach." And

Ruth and Cherry in cabaret.

so they formed a tunnel and we all ran through this tunnel to get on the coach.

Unbeknownst to any of us, this little guy was running behind us and leapt onto the coach with us. "Cherry, Cherry! I love you, Cherry!" It was most bizarre, as we hadn't noticed him follow us. A huge security bloke

just picked him up and threw him off the coach and I was devastated, thinking he was going to get killed.

Anyway, he was fine; he was waving at us as we left. They were all out of their minds… So drunk.

RUTH

Generally we recorded on a Wednesday and the programme went out on a Thursday. So Thursday, Friday and Saturday were usually the days we'd do cabaret. Some Thursdays we might get to a university gig, do our rehearsal, then creep into the Student Union where they were all watching *Top of the Pops* – because we wanted to see it too. And we'd be sitting there, and then the students would turn round and see us. And they wouldn't believe it was us. How could we be there?

BABS

One Thursday night we were up in Chester in a big barn with an audience of about 500 people. A fight broke out at the back, because there were some very unhappy people saying they'd paid good money to come and see Pan's People. But how *could* it be Pan's People when Pan's People were on television that evening?

SUE

Pan's People were a household name. They were very popular because they were the first of that kind. No one had ever created a dance group that was akin to a band. You could name these girls individually. You knew who they were, the same as you would know each member of The Beatles.

And we always appeared together. If one of the girls was ill or sick, then it would just be minus one. We never got replacements in. There were never stand-ins or understudies.

People did recognise us. When you were standing with Babs and everyone else, and you suddenly realised the reaction she'd spark in people, you'd think, "Gosh. People actually know these guys." And then

A promotional photo shoot at the seaside for the launch of Triang's sit-on Trundle Tanker toys.

you'd remember: "I'm one of them!" I suppose it could have been easy to lose our heads and think we were better than we were. But the nice thing about working with the girls was that they were very grounded.

CHERRY

These were the days when there were ten million viewers for every episode – just ridiculous. And we were always known individually. Sometimes we'd wear things with our names on them, or the DJs referred to us. So it wasn't just Pan's People. Everyone knew who we were individually.

STANLEY APPEL

I'm sure there were a great percentage of dads watching television that were only watching for Pan's People; I don't think they cared about anybody else. Once they'd seen Pan's People that was it, back to the radio.

They had an enormous fan base, and they were dearly loved. I don't know how it arose but every other day there was a photograph of one of the girls in the papers. Everybody knew Pan's People; school kids, dads, you name it. I think most people would be able to name, out of six, at least three or four of the girls. If, later on, you said to somebody "Name the girls that are in Legs & Co," I don't think they'd be able to do it.

PAUL SMITH

The impact that Pan's People had was massive. They replaced The Gojos, who were a much more sedate act; rather twee. Flick was much more aggressive in the choreography and the girls increasingly wore less and less in some of the routines. They were hugely popular. They were desired by young men, and I expect their fathers as well. And, equally, young women aspired to be like them. They were wholesome but couldn't help but be sexy too. They were great-looking girls.

ED STEWART

Top of the Pops was an essential part of people's lives. There was a two-year waiting list to be part of the audience. People based their social lives, their meal times and everything else around watching *Top of the Pops* on a Thursday night – it was a ritual. The viewing figures were huge. And Pan's People were part of it. A lot of people just watched for Pan's People, to see their dance routines and how gorgeous they looked. They were very, very popular. They were stars.

RUTH

I remember The Goodies taking us off. They did an all-pensioner dance troupe called 'Pan's Grannies'; that was hilarious. I went to the studio and was sitting in the audience when they played that film. It was so funny. I was just crying with laughter. I always think it's flattering when somebody takes the mickey. They were good friends of ours, and I always liked it when they were on *Top of the Pops*. In rehearsals, they always used to try and make us laugh and go wrong.

DEE DEE

We had lots of fan mail. A lot of it was from young girls who wanted to know if they could borrow our costumes, or maybe borrow the routines. A lot came from the forces – Navy, Army and Air Force – and we also had lovely letters from prisoners. I remember that one of the prisoners did this wonderful poster; it was a sort of paean to Pan's and how wonderful we all were. He used to write me wonderful poetry too.

We got letters from old-aged pensioners; from mothers who wanted to get something for their children; from young boys. But the core of our fan mail was from young males, who used to sit avidly watching *Top of the Pops* every Thursday night waiting for Pan's People to come on, hoping that we'd be wearing something very skimpy. I always remember Chris Tarrant saying that he used to go up to the television set and peer down the top of it to try and see down Babs' front.

CHERRY

We had fan mail from lots of kids, soldiers and people in the forces, and lots of women. And because of all the weird and wacky outfits that we wore from one week to the next, we got a lot of requests for "Where can I get…? Can I have the pattern for…? Would you mind, I need this for a wedding dress…" A lot of that went on, which was lovely. Then we had slightly more amorous ones, and lots of requests for pictures and all that kind of thing. On the whole it was lovely.

DEE DEE

We all had our special fans. I had one young lad, Billy Cameron, who worked in the cashmere company in Hawick. He used to send me wonderful sweaters and cashmeres, and then he started sending cashmeres

Pan's People's last Top of the Pops performance before Cherry's debut TV appearance – Ruth, Dee Dee, Louise and Babs dance to 'The Jean Genie' by David Bowie, 21 December 1972.

and sweaters to the other girls. And then if we had boyfriends, he'd send them sweaters too. He'd also send the boys bottles of whisky and things like that. He stayed my fan for years and years and years. Even when I got married and had children, he sent me knitted stuff for my children. Funnily enough, one of his red cardigans… I've still got it!

RUTH

Sometimes the fan mail was addressed to Pan's People, or sometimes they'd have a favourite. So it would be addressed to Dee Dee or Babs, care of Television Centre. We tried to handle the mail ourselves, but we just didn't have time to do it.

TESSA WATTS-RUSSELL

They trusted me to reply to their mail. It was mainly people asking for photographs; they had official photographs, which they usually signed. I had a Pan's People signature for the letters I wrote, which just said from Pan's People.

There were lots of young girls who were hoping to be a Pan's Person. Occasionally we'd invite them down to rehearsals. There were some who came along who'd managed to learn the routines just by watching them on television.

There were a few strange letters and I think most of them came via the *Top of the Pops* office. I think they maybe got opened before they came, but some didn't. I wasn't expected to respond to those. I think somebody else took those in hand.

PAUL SMITH

One of the jobs that I and the two production PAs had to do was go through the bagfuls of mail coming in every week addressed to Pan's People. The job was to sift out the ones which wouldn't be suitable to be read by the girls. Some young men had incredibly fertile imaginations and wanted to do all kinds of unmentionable things to them. The girls never saw the worst of them!

EIGHT
IN CONCERT
1973

★★★★★★★★★★★★★★★★★★★★★★★★★★★★★★★★★★★★

DEE DEE

December the 28th 1972 was Cherry's debut on *Top of the Pops*. She was wrapped up in a huge parcel. "I've got you the most beautiful Christmas present," said Tony Blackburn, and we unwrapped it in front of him. She was so nervous, the whole parcel shook.

CHERRY

My first *Top of the Pops*… I was terrified. I'd been on stage a thousand times, but you can rehearse until you're blue in the face – there's still something scary about actually being on TV for the first time. They wrapped me up as a Christmas parcel, and Tony Blackburn introduced me. The girls unwrapped me and out I came in this awful dress! I remember Flick saying years later, "What was I thinking with that dress?"

DEE DEE

We were wearing long, heavy dresses – virgin white – up to our necks and down to our feet, which obviously our male viewers weren't very happy about. And then we all danced to 'Without You' by Harry Nilsson.

CHERRY

The girls were very kind to me when I started, and incredibly protective. As a consequence, of course, I didn't have boyfriends or anything because everyone was terrified of us. A guy said to me years later, "I think I'd

OPPOSITE:
Ruth dances to Balinese bells in her solo segment of the In Concert *show.*

131

rather have had my arm cut off than try and approach Pan's People."
Nobody was brave enough to do it, which is a shame – and mad, really,
because we were all such nice girls.

RUTH

I think for anybody to approach us was very daunting. People used to
imagine we were inundated with male attention, but basically men were
too scared to approach us.

PAUL SMITH

They were almost untouchable. I was a relatively confident young lad and
my track record with women was fair to reasonable. But they were a
challenge. To ask one of Pan's People if they'd fancy going out for dinner?
My God, the pulse rate was at 170.

I asked Babs out once and she dealt with it absolutely brilliantly. We'd
got back from some filming and I said, "Babs, would you like to come to
dinner some time?" She just looked at me and kissed me on the cheek and
said, "Thank you, that's so lovely of you, Paul. But I've got a boyfriend
and I don't think he would like it."

It was such a nice way of saying "No, thank you."

CHERRY

I think we just naturally kept together as a group, and that made us quite
impenetrable. I remember Bryan Ferry from Roxy Music wanting to go
out with Dee Dee; he sent his minion over to invite her to dinner and all
that nonsense. But by and large we didn't get approached.

SUE

Because we spent so much time together, we did become almost like
family. We would often be working after the studios. And then maybe
going out for an evening meal, or we'd be going out and doing cabaret
and coming home at three o'clock in the morning. It wasn't like a nine-to-

five job, but it could sometimes take up a lot of the week.

BABS

It was very difficult to have relations outside of the group because the group came first. Working with Pan's People was all-encompassing. The work was what was important; the standard of work, the camaraderie, the team work and the friendships. There was never any in-fighting because we all had a single goal. We went to work like everybody else – to our rehearsal rooms, which were usually not terribly glamorous. We arrived in our rehearsal gear, we worked very hard through the day, and then we'd go home at night, get up the next morning and do it all over again.

A 1973 publicity photo by **Vogue** *photographer* **Richard Imrie.**

DEE DEE

We were a democracy, and we all made decisions, but when it came to business we were pretty useless. Jim Ramble had been good, but by this stage we were managing ourselves.

CHERRY

We ran ourselves. We each had a job in the group. It was very hokey, really. I was in charge of travel, Dee Dee was in charge of publicity, Babs was costumes. And Ruth did accounts. We all had our little jobs that we did. There were no merchandising deals that a manager would have put in place. We were paid £42 a week by the BBC, I seem to remember.

May 1973: in devil costumes on **The John Denver Show.**

SUE

I used to help out with costumes. I sort of helped out with everything really, as the group was self-sufficient. We didn't have people to do these things for us. We did it ourselves. So we all sort of chipped in.

We knew how we wanted things to work and who best to do it, rather than getting an outside person in to do these things. And it also gave us a bit of respect, because then people realised we weren't ditzy; we weren't airheads. We did have an agent, Dick Katz, who would get the initial jobs and bookings and things. But from there on in, it was run by us.

BABS

We were aware there were opportunities, but we didn't have the wherewithal to put them in place. And we didn't know anybody who could put them in place on our behalf. We were also concerned about being ripped off. We knew that there were possibilities, we knew there was potential to do things. But the problem was time and contacts.

DEE DEE

There were various people who wanted to manage us. And, in hindsight, I think it would have been better if we *had* had a manager. He would have taken an awful lot of money, but we would have also *made* a lot more money. Because everybody wanted to promote us in some way, from dolls to clothes, this and that and the other. But it never really happened.

CHERRY

There were no women in positions of power. The only one I remember was the *Blue Peter* producer Biddy Baxter. The women in our daily life would all be the costume designers and make-up artists and all that kind of thing. Apart from that, it was a very male-dominated set-up.

But we were very lucky. We had Stanley Dorfman, we had Robin Nash. We had all sorts of lovely old-school BBC producers who were very sympathetic to us. And, actually, they were all older. Everyone seemed old to me, I suppose!

BABS

I remember when the actor and political activist Corin Redgrave – Vanessa's brother – came to see us at our rehearsal rooms. He told us that their group were going to be outside the BBC with their Women's Liberation placards and asked if we'd boycott the show and march with them. And we said no. As far as we were concerned, we *were* liberated; we were doing what we wanted to do. We didn't see any point.

We did work at the time in a very male-orientated work place. The producers and directors, floor managers, cameramen, and sound and lighting technicians were all chaps. It was the receptionists, PAs and secretaries, make-up and costume people who were female, so I suppose the Redgraves had a point.

But having fought so hard to gain entry to and recognition at the BBC, we thought it better to demonstrate that we were, to a degree, independent and emancipated by working from within. We certainly didn't feel we had to hold up banners outside the BBC gates.

SUE

Sometimes we used to get a little flak from the female side of the audience. At our university gigs, for example, women would occasionally come out and say "Pan's People is all very sexist."

If anything, it was the opposite. Every area and element of how we worked was done by ourselves. We decided what we wanted to do. We were very much in charge of ourselves, very much in control and we didn't actually need men to do that. So we weren't exactly letting the female side down.

BABS

What they didn't take into account was the fact that we were a team of women running our own lives. We were doing what we wanted to do, the way we wanted to do it.

SUE

Nothing ever stopped a show. Everyone was entitled to their opinion, but nothing would stop us from going on. By and large, there was no problem. And anyway, when the complainers actually saw our gigs, they realised it wasn't what they first thought. It wasn't titillation, it was entertainment. So after a while they actually got it – and backed off.

We were interviewed at the time and I think it was Ruth who said, "Look. This isn't a sexist show. We're completely in charge of our act. We do what we want. We're not sex slaves to the male population."

RUTH

We quite often had women trying to stop our performances at the
university gigs. Glasgow was the one I particularly remember. We did an
interview on their local student radio station, and they were trying to say
we were just puppets under male control.

Our argument was that it was completely the opposite. We were in
charge of our own lives; in fact, we employed two men. One was the
sound guy and the other was our driver. So we were, in fact, more
Women's Lib than they were.

Which in the long run – when I look back – wasn't completely true. As
far as the BBC went, we were caught by the short and curlies. Ultimately,
we weren't as independent as we thought we were.

BABS

It was in March 1973 that the *Frankie Howerd in Ulster* special was shown
on BBC1. This was something we'd done just before Christmas; it was all
organised by the BBC. We flew out to Belfast and did our rehearsals.
Frankie literally raised the roof. The troops adored him. He was very
funny. He gave us a wonderful introduction; massive great cheer from the
lads. But again, just like in 1969, we never spoke.

PAUL SMITH

It was soon after the Troubles had started, so it was decided by the
powers-that-be that there should be a show to entertain the troops. I had
to charter an aircraft, which was very unusual at the time. We set the
whole thing up in a big hangar at Aldergrove airport in Belfast and the
troops came along there. Frankie Howerd was topping the bill and Pan's
People were providing the glam.

DEE DEE

We danced in Belfast in an enormous aircraft hangar. When we came out
to do the number, the applause was so thunderous we couldn't hear our

Celebrating the 500th edition of **Top of the Pops** *with DJs Tony Blackburn, Kenny Everett and Noel Edmonds, plus singer Lynsey de Paul and Roxy Music members Paul Thompson, Phil Manzanera and Eddie Jobson – 22 November 1973.*

cue. How we actually picked it up I don't know. But when you've got maybe a thousand men in uniform, screaming and shouting and whistling, it's very difficult to hear the music. It was the most tremendous reception I think we ever had.

RUTH

When the curtain went up there were all these young soldiers sitting in front of us – in combat gear, with their rifles and everything. It took my breath away. I nearly froze. At any moment, they could just up and go. It was so shocking; they were really young. Even to us.

DEE DEE

Even though we were dancing, we could still see out into the audience. We could see the boys in uniform, and a lot of them had their guns sitting beside them, just sitting at their side. It was quite poignant.

It was a dangerous place. But we didn't think about things like that. It didn't bother me, anyway. I thought that we were going to entertain the troops and we were going to have a lot of fun.

PAUL SMITH

It didn't scare me at all because I knew that we'd be well guarded and looked after by the troops themselves and by the security forces there. But it was a daunting prospect for many of the people on the bill who had never been to Northern Ireland, and everybody had to volunteer.

RUTH

At one point, while we were doing our rehearsals, we were told that we mustn't, on any account, run anywhere. But it was pouring with rain and we just instinctively ran.

BABS

I was running across the parade ground one time, looking for the loo, when I got a tap on the shoulder. It was a guard with a gun. "Don't run! You could get shot!" He wasn't joking.

CHERRY

Early in my time with Pan's I had a couple of really weird things happen to me, unfortunately.

I would have been 18 at the time, and I'd just moved into a little flat on my own. I'd originally shared a place with some friends from the Royal Ballet Company, but then the opportunity arose to have a little flat in Chiswick, through someone I knew.

I'd just moved there when one day I got a call from the CID. "Are you alone? Can we come and see you?" So they came to see me and said, "You're not to get worried, but the BBC has contacted us and they've received two threats about you. One is a kidnap threat and the other is a murder threat."

Which was a little bit scary.

But they said, "Now listen. Before you get worried, in our experience whenever someone is brazen enough to say 'I'm going to do this and I'm going to do that', in our experience it never happens. It's the ones that you don't know about that you have to be scared of."

But obviously I had to take major precautions. Don't give your number out. Don't do this, don't do that, don't do the other. It coincided with a spate of obscene phone calls I'd been receiving. It wasn't a question of randomly phoning a number. These people definitely knew who I was. So that was fairly scary as well.

No one could understand it. I was ex-directory. We were super-scrupulous about security. And we weren't swanning about town; we were basically just busy working. The only people who knew my details were the people that would collect me. Black cabs, mini-cabs, limo drivers taking us to cabaret shows. Just people you thought you completely trusted.

Immediately you think, "Can I trust my friends? Can I trust this person? Can I trust that one?" It was a bit weird, I have to say.

Anyway, the CID followed me closely for a while, and I didn't have any more problems. Then some time later, we were all sitting round, going through our BBC scripts, when I realised that the details of every single person involved in the production of the show – technicians, performers, everyone – were printed on the front of this script. So basically anybody that had been passing through on the day of a *Top of the Pops* recording could have picked up one of these scripts and passed on the information.

So our contact details were pretty much public knowledge. It really wasn't the mystery we all thought it was.

TESSA WATTS-RUSSELL

Soon after the Frankie Howerd special went out the group did *The John Denver Show* for BBC2, which was maybe the strangest one of all.

It was all about magic; there was a wizard and a frog involved. The floor manager had heavy gloves to hold the frog with and had to put it on a cushion. And I said, "You can't do that, the poor frog." And they let me hold the frog and just take my hands away at the vital moment. Which I was happy to do, because I absolutely adore frogs.

John gave us all a necklace with aspen leaves on it as a thank-you present at the end of the series. I still wear it every day, just because it was such a nice thing to do.

Louise dances with the US star on **The John Denver Show.**

BABS

John was a little bit like Bobbie Gentry. I don't think he had natural dancing ability. But he did have great enthusiasm and charm. We did quite

Dancing with dogs in an iconic Pan's People performance of Gilbert O'Sullivan's 'Get Down' on the 1973 Top of the Pops Christmas Special.

a lot of location filming with him. I remember him buying us all ice creams when we were filming down by Waterloo Bridge.

I actually had a knee injury and thought I wasn't going to be able to do the shows. But it was suggested I go to Chelsea Football Club, where the sports therapists were wonderful and soon sorted the problem out. Thanks to them I did manage to perform in the last couple of shows. Also, Flick ensured that I was in all of the shows, even if it was only audience participation rather than an energetic dance routine, just so that I'd get paid.

CHERRY

We also did a series with The Two Ronnies in late '73, early '74. We didn't have an awful lot to do with them, but we'd see them when we ran through the show at the BBC rehearsal studios. And then the next time we'd see them would probably be in the studio. But they were divine, completely and utterly. Incredibly disciplined, incredibly talented, and very sweet with us. Just real old-school fabulousness.

DEE DEE

The biggest thing that happened to us in '73, though, was being given our own *In Concert* programme.

In Concert was a BBC2 series, produced and directed by Stanley Dorfman, which always featured a single artist over half an hour. Flick came to us and said that Pan's People were going to be given their own show. It was unheard of for a group of dancers to get an *In Concert* so we felt incredibly rewarded for all our hard work.

A lot of 1973 was spent working towards this big moment. We finally recorded it on New Year's Eve at the Shepherd's Bush Theatre. We'd done the famous *Top of the Pops* routine to Gilbert O'Sullivan's 'Get Down' – with all those dogs – just the week before.

STANLEY DORFMAN

In Concert was originally about song writing. Leonard Cohen was in town, so we called the first one *Leonard Cohen sings Leonard Cohen*. Then Bill Cotton thought for a bit and said it would be a nice idea to do a series on songwriters and call each one *Joni Mitchell sings Joni Mitchell* and so forth. But then I was reading the Sunday paper one day and I saw the headline 'Yehudi Menuhin in Concert at the Royal Festival Hall'. And I thought, "That's a great title!" So it became *In Concert*.

CHERRY

In Concert was an iconic show. It was incredibly flattering to be considered as a band, if you like. I think there were several things that Flick had always wanted to do – pieces of music she wanted to incorporate without being confined to the Top 20 and all that entails.

RUTH

It was a bit like *The Old Grey Whistle Test* but with just one artist in concert, doing their thing. Some wonderful people were on that series. I remember being in the audience with Flick for the Elton John edition in 1970.

To have our own show was a really big deal for us. Because we worked so quickly, it was a real luxury to have time to create and rehearse something else, and to show the variety of things we could do. Although I do remember we weren't always 100 per cent keen on what Flick chose for us.

STANLEY DORFMAN

Flick constructed it. She chose the music, and then we'd build sets for every dance routine. And again she very much directed it through me, telling me which shots would go to which cameras.

DEE DEE

Flick was able to go to town with her routines, because Stan told her she could do anything she liked. So each girl had a number of her own to dance to. I drew the short straw, unfortunately. All the other girls got wonderful solo numbers to do, but I got to dance to a poem which was read by BBC director Roger Ordish. I wasn't very happy, I must admit.

RUTH

I did a number to Balinese bells. They don't have the same musical structure that we're used to, so on the first day of rehearsal Flick and I spent ages trying to figure out where we were going to start and finish. It was like learning something completely alien. I remember that the set looked like half a tulip. And my hair was wrapped up around a toilet roll, not that anybody knew that. It was really difficult, because of the structure of the music, but I think the end result was very beautiful.

DEE DEE

We had to tap dance and sing to an old Max Bygraves song, 'Smile'.

Unfortunately Pan's People couldn't do either. We did have a couple of tappers amongst us, Louise and Babs, so they kept us going and the rest of us just faked it.

Although we looked quite cute, it was just awful, because we were singing in high-pitched voices and then tapping very badly. I think if any other dancers were watching, they were probably laughing. There were moments when Flick did things with us that didn't really work, to be honest.

But then there were other numbers which were fantastic. 'Willow Weep for Me' was just a wonderful number, as was the opening song, 'Let's Face the Music and Dance' by Ella Fitzgerald.

The opening number of In Concert, *'Let's Face the Music and Dance'.*

CHERRY

My number was 'My Father', a beautiful song by Judy Collins. We were all fairly nervous. I'd like to have done more takes on some things, but you never really feel you perfect anything.

DEE DEE

My least favourite number was the last one, 'LA Resurrection' by Buddy Miles. We wore these tops and bottoms which had hanging balls on them, and every time we moved these balls would drop off onto the set. And then, whilst we were dancing and gyrating and doing turns, the balls would bash us in the stomach or the bum and so on. They weren't very comfortable costumes to wear.

RUTH

I loathed the last number with whistles. There was another one that was a bit bizarre and avant-garde, crawling around to noises. It was more like an art installation, and it didn't quite work. I knew what Flick was trying to do but I thought it was a little pretentious.

DEE DEE

We started off with one of us asleep – I think it was me. And then we danced to all the sounds that you would hear during a working day. I thought it was quite good, and very inventive of Flick.

RUTH

The standout performance was obviously Louise and Dee Dee and the cushions. It was one of the sexiest things ever.

BABS

Dee Dee and Louise's routine was particularly saucy. The costumes were probably the most expensive the BBC had ever paid for, but they were literally just backless bikinis – two bejewelled shells and a little bikini

*Louise and Dee Dee's famous dance on the cushions for **In Concert**.*

bottom. The set was decorated with cushions on which the girls moved and it was lit with huge candles. It was a very sultry routine, but I don't think anyone other than Mary Whitehouse found it offensive.

DEE DEE

Louise and I did our famous dance on the cushions, live in front of the theatre audience. We wore very little, but they were the most expensive costumes the BBC had ever made for us. There were so many beads and intricate details on these tiny bikinis that we took up the whole of the budget for the week on just these two costumes.

We were just writhing around on some cushions, and I think the male population enjoyed that particular routine. Though I have to say that Louise was the star of the show. Louise just oozed sex appeal. She had this wonderful face with very broad cheekbones and beautiful eyes, and this cascade of majestic hair. I'm not saying that I didn't look gorgeous too! But I think, of the two of us, she passed the winning post first on that particular number.

RUTH

I was the first one to record, and was terribly nervous. I was so nervous I was shaking. I could see myself shake when I watched it back. I would've loved to have done it again but I didn't have that luxury.

DEE DEE

For some ridiculous reason, December the 31st was chosen as the day we should actually film the show. I think it was very nice of the audience to come and spend two or three hours of their New Year's Eve in a stuffy theatre, watching various technical problems and us getting things either right or wrong.

BABS

We kept running over on certain things. And at the end of a very long day we still needed more time. Stanley phoned down to the boys in VT and said, "Look. Can we have another half hour? If that's all right. I know it's New Year's Eve…" And they said, "Fine." We still needed more time, so he rang down again. And they just said, "Look. Don't call again. Just keep going until you're happy and you've got the show in the can. Just tell us when we can go home!"

They were just wonderful, those boys. The sound, all the technicians, the cameramen, make-up, wardrobe – everybody was so behind the project. It was such a wonderful feeling of unity and collaboration – what television really should be about.

RUTH

I remember the relief when it was all over. We rushed to Louise's flat at Grosvenor House and had a New Year's Eve party.

BABS

Louise and her boyfriend Tony Dobson had an apartment at the Grosvenor House Hotel. And they threw a party, for parents and friends and family. There was a little plate of blinis going round and my brother-in-law ate a whole plateful. He'd never eaten caviar before and didn't know it was such a delicacy. He probably cost Tony a fortune!

DEE DEE

We'd tried to do the *In Concert* show as much as possible as a live performance, but we also recorded a couple of things that were slotted in later. One of them was a lovely number which had very lyrical, sexy music. We had wonderful long skirts and tops that were completely see-through. And of course we didn't wear bras in those days.

When we filmed that particular number, the studio was full of men. Absolutely chock-a-block. But you were only allowed a certain amount of people in the studio at any one time, thanks to fire regulations, so the director had to send everybody out.

For me, rehearsing and performing *In Concert* was the most wonderful time. There's so much that you put into learning to dance. It's very very difficult. You have to get up early in the morning and go into cold studios and put yourself through a lot of pain. And then when you become a dancer, most of the time you're shoved under the doormat – because dancers aren't considered anything wonderful, they're just a little bit of icing on the cake.

So for us it was a fantastic moment to actually be recognised for our art. In some ways, it was the climax of Pan's People. Nothing quite so wonderful happened to us after that.

BABS

Yes. To have our own *In Concert* show at the BBC… I'd say that was the pinnacle of our career.

NINE
YOU CAN REALLY ROCK AND ROLL ME
1974

★★★★★★★★★★★★★★★★★★★★★★★★★★★★★★★★★★★★★★

DEE DEE

In January 1974 we did *The Jack Jones Show*, for Stanley Dorfman again.

Jack Jones was an American crooner who came over here in the '70s. He wasn't very friendly and was the meanest man you could ever meet. It's sort of traditional that, at the end of filming a show, the artists you're working for throw a little party or give everybody a small present. And at the end of this show, I think we bought him a gold cigarette lighter and presented it to him. But he didn't give anybody anything. Nothing at all. He also never carried money, so if we filmed outside he would never buy you a drink or anything like that, because he didn't have any money on him.

In any case, he was having this raging affair with the actress Susan George, so wasn't interested in us particularly.

CHERRY

Jack and Susan had big rows. We were in a dressing room with them when they chose to have a row one time. It was one of those really embarrassing "Beam me up, Scotty" moments. Just get me out of here! One of those.

RUTH

We were rehearsing for *The Jack Jones Show* in this grotty rehearsal room

OPPOSITE:
Sue (front centre) replaced Louise in May 1974 and made her TV debut the following month.

151

on Scrubs Lane, near Wormwood Scrubs prison. It was freezing cold; so cold that we were dancing in our coats and gloves around a gas heater the BBC had given us. We hadn't met Jack at that point, so Stanley Dorfman brought him in to meet us. After they'd gone we looked in the mirror and saw we had dirt from the heater all over our faces. I don't know what Jack must have thought. "So much for my glamorous dancers," probably. He gave us a wide berth for a little while.

DEE DEE

Jack did this number called 'Baubles, Bangles and Beads' and they actually rigged an enormous bath in the studios. We were dressed as his handmaidens, he was dressed up – if I remember rightly – in a turban, and we were actually in this bath with him.

We had nothing on up top, just beads mischievously covering our nipples. It was supposed to be warm, but when you film something as elaborate as that you don't do just one take. So after a while the water became absolutely freezing. A lot of it was filmed from the back, so you saw our naked backs with lots of hair.

Flick was very daring in that sort of situation. Nothing like that had ever been done before, dancers with next to nothing on.

BABS

We were contracted to do six Jack Jones shows, but only four of the six were recorded because of a union strike. We were still paid.

DEE DEE

As young people we weren't that aware of what was going on in politics and everything else. I vaguely remember the Three Day Week. But life was just one great big laugh. It was great fun.

BABS

I was conscious of the strikes at the time, but I don't think we were really

'Dance with the Devil' by Cozy Powell, Top of the Pops, 13 December 1973.

affected by them that much.

Talking of strikes, there was another show we did in the very early days. It was a one-off ATV special with Jerry Lee Lewis and there was some kind of technicians' strike. But as we had a studio audience, Jerry decided to go ahead and perform the show anyway, but with no cameras. It was a really exciting show and the energy levels in the studio were electric. But it was strange doing a show and seeing the still cameras. It was so sad that the show was never recorded, and never broadcast.

DEE DEE

In February 1974 Jimmy Savile was doing a series called *Clunk-Click*. It was a show that was based around safety for children. I think the government had introduced legislation that seat belts should be worn, and Jimmy's show was somehow connected to that.

We were invited onto the show to chat to him. We were wearing very beautiful, long, black sequinned dresses which were slit all the way up to the top of the thigh. They were almost backless and halter-necked, and slit right down to the waist. And the only way we could keep our boobs from falling out was by using toupée tape.

Jimmy was sitting in his famous chair, and we were all sitting on either side of him. I thought we were quite charming, but Mary Whitehouse, who was the self-appointed campaigner for keeping television clean, went ballistic. She said, "How dare Jimmy Savile have Pan's People on at 6.00 pm – with young children watching – when they're wearing such disgusting costumes?"

I didn't agree with her at all; we looked absolutely beautiful.

We picked up the papers the next day and there was all this talk about it. And of course there were pictures of us everywhere. That was the ironic thing – Mary Whitehouse just made us more popular. I don't think she liked us very much. She felt we were there just to titillate and tantalise men.

CHERRY

Mary Whitehouse was a regular complainer. There was an issue with white trousers once, about whether they were see-through. I also remember there was one costume that somebody only pointed out years later. We did a Barry White routine and we were in white leotards and tights, with huge hats. But some bright spark did a slow-motion version of it and, of course, they were completely see-through. Luckily, nobody at the time realised, so we got away with it. Mary Whitehouse didn't notice that one!

BABS

There were some raunchy routines, and there were some sexy costumes, but I don't think we ever wore anything that was particularly offensive. Except to Mary Whitehouse of course, who basically felt that we should be banned from TV.

CHERRY

I don't think we thought of ourselves as sexy. We were very naïve in that way. The only time I remember thinking "Bloody hell!" is when Louise and Dee Dee did their cushion number on *In Concert*. If Mary Whitehouse had been watching she probably would've had a heart attack on the spot. I remember thinking, "Crumbs. This is a bit near the knuckle, girls."

STANLEY APPEL

When they had to dance to something that had a bit of bite to it, it got a little raunchier – but they got away with it. There was never sex as such. But the fact that they were good-looking girls helped.

DEE DEE

Although we were good dancers, we were also pretty girls with lovely figures, and that was one of the reasons people enjoyed watching us. Our male fans weren't really that interested in the routines or costumes. In fact, they used to complain if we had costumes right up to our necks and showed nothing at all.

CHERRY

When Arlene Phillips' group Hot Gossip came along, it highlighted the fact that Pan's had always been flirtatious and ladylike, as opposed to explicit and brazen. They were a bit more ITV. We were still at the BBC, don't forget.

DEE DEE

In May 1974 Louise left Pan's People. She was in love with Tony Dobson, who lived up in Sheffield, and it became a question of either Pan's or Tony. And Louise rightly chose Tony.

Tony was a wealthy entrepreneur whom we met at a gig at Grosvenor House. It was Louise's 21st birthday and they were together from that

Ruth, Louise, Dee Dee and Babs on horseback during one of their weekly rides with Ruth's father George.

moment on. He was a northerner and dressed quite beautifully; he always had the most incredible outfits. But he was one of these no-nonsense guys who felt "It's either me or the dancing." Louise was totally, totally besotted by him, so it was the right decision for her.

RUTH

Tony wanted her to be up there with him in Sheffield and they wanted to have a family. She used to commute for a while, which was just ridiculous. And then Louise just announced it to us one day. I think we were all in denial a bit. We should have realised. For myself, anyway, it came as a shock. But really it made sense.

DEE DEE

When she told us she was leaving, I suppose our first reaction was that we were being let down.

We felt, "God, you're leaving us? You're leaving the group?" Because the one thing about Pan's is that we've been through fights, we've had our arguments, we've gossiped about each other, but at the end of the day there is this incredible bond. As a group we were always there for each other, and we were incredibly strong as a unit. And suddenly one of the formative members was leaving. I thought, "You can't do that! You can't leave us. We've got more to do."

Very selfish of me I know, but it's how I felt at that moment.

CHERRY

Louise leaving was a shame, because at that point I think we had such a great line-up. She was an incredibly popular member of the group. When I watched *Top of the Pops*, she was my favourite. I thought she was fairly iconic.

DEE DEE

Personally speaking, I think it left a big void in Pan's. Because one of the attractions of Pan's was that we were all so individual.

Ruthie was sort of sultry and eastern-looking, I was the mad bubbly one, Babs was the blonde bombshell, the very pretty one was Cherry. And then there was this goddess called Louise, who just oozed sex appeal. She just had to slightly smile or do a hip movement and that was it really.

And, of course, then we held auditions for her replacement.

SUE

From the age of four-and-a-half, dancing was the one thing that I wanted to do. I wanted to be Margot Fonteyn, no two ways about it.

I was born in Africa, in Benghazi, in September 1955. My father was in the army and he was stationed out there at the time I was born. We were fondly referred to as 'army brats' because, wherever Mum and Dad went, we went with them. My mother was German and my father was English;

they'd met in Hamburg during the war and had fallen in love. We stayed in Africa for about two years or so and then moved to Farnborough in Hampshire.

Aged four, I went along to the local ballet school, the Mayfair School of Dancing, with my sister Jane. My mother thought Jane, who was five years older than me, would enjoy dancing. But she hated it; all she wanted to do was ride horses and become a vet. I loved it, so I learnt tap and ballet and character dancing from different countries. I did a lot of competitions and dance festivals, in Farnborough, in Woking, in Kent, in London – all over the place. I remember seeing Cherry in one of the competitions, doing 'A Windmill in Old Amsterdam' dressed up as a mouse. She was very cute and won first place.

At the age of ten, I auditioned for the Arts Educational Ballet School in Tring and went to the boarding school there – the old Rothschild mansion – till I was 16. There were 250 girls boarding, seven days a week, morning, noon and night. I loved it and ended up as head girl, which made my mum proud. When I left, I was going to finish my training and then look for work – in ballet. At that time, they had a student part of Arts Educational at the Barbican, so I went there for the last two years to finish off my exams.

Sue at age seven with a dance trophy.

It was at that point, at the end of the first year, that I started to get terrible trouble with my feet; when I was doing point work at the barre, my toes would get stuck. It was then that I was told I had arthritis in my toe joints.

So I became completely distraught, thinking, "That's it. I'll never dance again."

But the osteopath who was treating me said, "Have you ever thought of changing the *style* of dance that you're doing?"

So I started doing more contemporary work and really enjoyed it. I used to do lessons at the Dance Centre in Covent Garden, where Arlene Phillips was my jazz teacher. Babs and Flick were auditioning to find a replacement for Louise but couldn't find anyone they were happy with, so one day so they sat in on one of Arlene's jazz classes. At the end they introduced themselves and said, "Would you like to come along and do an afternoon with Flick to see how you get on?"

I went along to their rehearsal room, which was in a very tatty part of Holland Park. It was an old sports hall with a huge glass window on one side of the room. The girls had just finished rehearsing a number for *Top of the Pops* – 'Spiders and Snakes' by Jim Stafford. It was just me and two, maybe three other girls who'd been picked from other schools by the other ladies. And we went through this routine and Flick kept making us go over it and over it. The Pan's People girls were all watching from outside, which was really nerve-wracking. And at the end of it, Flick went out and had a word with them.

I think they decided then, "Yep. We'll give Sue a try." And that was that.

Interestingly, a week after being spotted in the jazz class by Babs and Flick, I was supposed to have auditioned for a classical and contemporary ballet company in Gras, Switzerland… So things could have turned out very differently for me!

RUTH

I remember Susie being very shy and very very nervous. It must have been pretty daunting, and understandably she was quite intimidated by the whole thing.

Like Cherry, she had to learn on the job, because they were both young and went right in at the top. We learnt a lot of our craft abroad, before we ever worked in England. But they suddenly came in – young and inexperienced – to a very famous group, on television every week. It's a hell of a lot to cope with. And to work under that pressure.

But once she'd calmed down a bit, Susie was an incredible dancer, she really was.

SUE

Louise did her last performance on the 16th of May – R Dean Taylor's 'There's a Ghost in My House'. I was introduced to viewers by Dave Lee Travis on the same show. I was just standing there next to him; I didn't say anything. It was all a bit gobsmacking, to be honest. It all seemed a bit surreal.

My first performance followed on the 6th of June and was the most nerve-wracking thing I think I've ever done. We danced to The Isley Brothers' 'Summer Breeze', which was a lovely routine and a lovely song. But I was shaking like a leaf, I was so nervous. I remember thinking, "I'm going to make a really big mistake and fall flat on my face." But I didn't. It was over so quickly that I almost couldn't remember doing it. It was fine. And it went out and I thought, "Gosh. That's the start of it."

And then the unions went out on strike! So it was about seven weeks before viewers saw me again. In other words, I had seven weeks to get it right! I still had to get used to working with cameras. We used to have rehearsals during the afternoon where we learnt the camera positions. Flick would actually script the cameras herself and would tell us, "I'm coming towards you. So at this point in the routine, try not to look the other way. And look towards the camera and smile. And try and look nice."

It was a big learning curve for me. It's not the most natural thing to suddenly turn round and find a camera shooting right up your bum or right in your face or what have you. So that took some getting used to.

These girls had worked together for years. Even Cherry had worked with them a good 18 months longer than I had. So they were all used to each other. For me, it was very different. I was 18, straight out of boarding school, and I'd never done anything like this. And it took a while, you know. Flick was a taskmaster. And I remember shedding a few tears,

Sue joins Babs for the opening of a fête at RAF Coningsby in Lincolnshire.

thinking, "I'm never going to get this right." And her saying, "Stop the tears, just get on with it."

And that was the best thing for me. I respected her for that, and I hope she respected me for sticking with it and really trying to make an effort.

But it took me a while to settle into the group, I have to say. Because they were all stunning, iconic girls; all were known as sex symbols. It took a while, but they were so supportive. They all helped me, in every sense: from settling into the group from the dancing point of view to dealing with being in the public eye. They were really really kind – very protective and understanding.

I used to live in the Barbican when I was still a student. So at the end of

Flick at a **Top of the Pops** *rehearsal.*

rehearsals, Babs used to very kindly drop me off at the Barbican, and my friends would always say "Wow!" I could never work out whether they were impressed by the fact that I was being driven home by Babs from Pan's People, or the fact that she had this really cool white MG.

CHERRY

Going forward, Sue was a great addition. That period, 1974 and '75, was really the height of our popularity.

SUE

It was all very friendly on *Top of the Pops*. David Bowie was there. The Sweet, Status Quo, Stevie Wonder, Queen. Cliff Richard was there; he was always there. All the Slade lot, all the Mud lot, all the Sweet lot. All of the bands, really, would always come up and say "Hi." And then after the show there was the BBC bar where everyone used to have a drink afterwards. The bands would come up there and we'd all sit round and have a laugh.

CHERRY

I was sitting next to Keith Moon in make-up one day. And he had this terrible mark on the end of his nose, so I eventually said, "I've got to ask, what happened to your nose?" And he said, "Oh, someone stubbed out a cigarette on it."

SUE

There was no standoff-ishness. You're just all normal people at the end of the day. David Bowie was such a nice, normal person. It's one thing when you're on stage. When you come off stage, you're a normal human being. You still go home, still do the washing up and everything else. You're all just people.

I suppose Freddie Mercury used to be a little bit diva-ish. But then that was just his outrageous manner, the way he was. But I can't remember anyone really being a diva as such. Because *Top of the Pops* wouldn't tolerate it. It was a case of "We're doing you a favour because you're promoting your band, your single. If you want to get on in the charts, then you just do it the way we do it."

The artists obviously knew the girls, and would always say "Hi." They never overstepped the mark with the girls. There's something intimidating about six women.

CHERRY

I remember Stevie Wonder's band being on; they played live in the studio. And it was so exciting that Robin Nash – who was the producer of the show at that time – stopped the show and came down on the studio floor from the box. He walked up onto the set in his bow tie and said, "You have no idea what a privilege this is. Could you play something else for us?"

Stevie threw his head back and laughed, and went into the opening bars of 'Superstition'. The place went insane. I remember thinking, "My God, this is so exciting." Then the rest of the day, I seemed to be running from Stevie's drummer, who for some reason had taken a shine to me and followed me all round the studio.

Another one I remember was Bing Crosby. He must have been ancient at the time; it must have been one of the very last things he did. He was on a stool and we were on just after him. We were all standing there waiting to perform and when they came to take him off the stool he said, "Who's this?" And they said, "Oh, this is Pan's People." He said, "Leave me here. I think this is something I need to see."

So he stayed sitting on his stool and watched us do our routine. Great fun.

SUE

Those were the wonderful days of platform shoes. We used to wear these wedges. And heels that were equally high. We'd have these beautiful platform go-go silver boots. They weren't dainty footwear, far from it. They were clumpy. So that used to make a difference to the dancing. There was a lot to take on board and try to get right. And obviously the most important bit was to try not to sweat too much, because your costume was only stuck on with double-sided sticky tape!

DEE DEE

It was in 1974 that I was injured for three months. By then the glam rock scene was at its height, and platform heels were very much the norm. I was rehearsing in a pair of black and silver high-heeled platform shoes, and I fell off them and pulled all the ligaments in my ankle. For the next three months I couldn't dance, so there were only four girls in the Pan's routines at that time. That was terrible for me because I really felt it was the beginning of the end.

I lost an enormous amount of confidence because of my leg; there was always the fear of having to give up dancing. And what would I do then?

Luckily, my parents were back in the country and were very supportive. My mother took me to a faith healer, which helped me enormously. And eventually, trouper that I was, I came back.

After that, most of the time when I did a show I'd do it with my ankle strapped up. A lot of people weren't looking at our feet, so I don't think anyone noticed. But that was another reason why I left at the end of 1975, because my ankle really wasn't bearing up to some of the rigorous dancing we were doing.

BABS

It was September 1974 when I was mentioned in an episode of *Porridge*. As Fletch, Ronnie Barker said, "I could ring up a couple of birds, you know. Couple of them darlings that dance on *Top of the Pops*, you know what I mean? What are they called? Pan's People, yeah. There's one special one. Beautiful Babs. Dunno what her name is."

It was a terrific compliment. In fact, Ronnie came up to me in the BBC bar after he recorded that particular show and said, "I'm awfully sorry, but we used your name in the programme. What I wanted to say was 'Big Babs', but the producer wouldn't let me. I think 'Big Babs' would've been funnier."

And I said, "Well, I think you're right, and I wouldn't have been offended at all."

I told him it was an honour to be mentioned in his show. Many people have come up to me since and said "Did you know that Ronnie Barker mentioned you on *Porridge*?" It's one that's stayed with me through the decades.

DEE DEE

Around August that year, we did our ill-fated single 'You Can Really Rock and Roll Me' – by Mike Batt of Wombles fame. It was released through one of CBS' smaller labels, Epic.

CHERRY

Yes, somebody had the bright idea for us to make a single. "Oh yes, let's do that. Of course…"

A signed promotional photo for 'You Can Really Rock and Roll Me'.

DEE DEE

It was a good little number but, of course, none of us could really sing. Cherry was the only one who could sing at all.

BABS

Cherry had a very good singing voice, but if we'd carried on we'd have needed some pretty serious voice coaching. I am not renowned for even singing in the bath.

SUE

The record company thought, "It's obvious. It's a no-brainer. We've got the dance group that works on that pop programme. Why don't we bring a single out?"

Mike Batt had two songs for us. One was the old Rolling Stones song 'The Singer Not the Song', which became the B-side. The other was 'You Can Really Rock and Roll Me', which Mike wrote himself. So we went into the studio to see who had the best voice, and it was Cherry.

CHERRY

I remember being in the studio. I was quite used to being in a studio, because at the time I was doing some backing vocals for my then partner. So I wouldn't have been particularly thrown by it.

RUTH

Cherry sang one verse and I did another verse. I was so nervous, they had to get somebody to go to the pub next door and get a port and brandy for me. It was a long day. Cherry could sing, I couldn't.

DEE DEE

We worked our little arses off to promote it. We did a record company convention down in Eastbourne alongside Leonard Cohen. It was Leonard Cohen, The Three Degrees, David Essex and a group called Sailor – with a young lad in it called Henry, my future husband. And we actually got up and performed 'You Can Really Rock and Roll Me'. We did so much publicity on that blasted record. So, not for want of trying, it should have done well in the charts.

The BBC, however, absolutely refused to let us perform it on the show. We never really understood why they refused to promote us when they were very happy to promote another dance group from the BBC, a spin-off from The Young Generation called Feet First. We were seething; we felt terribly betrayed. The song did enter the charts, but when we didn't get our moment on *Top of the Pops* it just sank without trace. We did everything possible to make it work and the BBC just dug their heels in and said "No!"

CHERRY

It never occurred to any of us that the BBC wouldn't be allowed to play our single. Because it would be seen as payola – promoting a BBC artist on BBC radio and TV. So it was all a bit of a waste of time. Nobody really thought it through.

RUTH

There was a lot of prejudice. People wouldn't let you do more than one thing if you were well known. If you were a dancer, you weren't taken seriously as a singer. So there was an element of that. And I don't think it was promoted properly. I think if the record company had really been behind us, they could have done more.

DEE DEE

We did another single, 'He's Got Magic', with 'Sooner or Later' as the B-side. Like the first one, it bombed out of the charts – not for want of trying. We really did an awful lot of promotion for it, especially up north. We'd go around the country and perform the record in shopping malls.

But it was all too much. If we'd ever done well and if they'd asked us to do an album, I think I would've lost the will to live and jumped off a cliff. Luckily, it didn't happen.

SUE

You may be good with your feet, but you're not necessarily brilliant with your voice. I think we realised it was best to stick with what we did best – which was dancing. None of us were great singers. We were adequate. No more than that.

DEE DEE

It was in November of 1974 that we did a few nights at the Rainbow Theatre with Jethro Tull. It was called 'The Grand London Return Concert'. For some reason, Stirling Moss, the racing driver, was the compere of the show; don't ask me why. Ian Anderson was the lead vocalist. He had frizzy hair and a goatee beard and he used to stand on one leg and play the flute while wearing a codpiece.

IAN ANDERSON
JETHRO TULL

I was looking to have a few guests on the show, and I suppose like most men between the ages of 12 and 65 I couldn't take my eyes off Pan's People on *Top of the Pops*. We all knew who they were. They were the highlight of a pretty dreary show, cavorting with a sort of provocative innocence.

When I approached Flick I think she was concerned at first that we might be manipulative rock stars. But I presented her with a tune that I'd written and she warmed to the idea. It gave them the opportunity to do something that was more choreographed and balletic than their usual three minutes on *Top of the Pops*. They got quite into it.

SUE

We did three numbers there. We did 'Witches Promise', 'Living in the Past' and Ian actually wrote a piece on pan pipes for us. Ian and Terry Ellis, Jethro Tull's manager, had thought of the idea, and we obviously had to do a couple of numbers from their album. But Ian also said, "I'd like to do a piece for the girls. What do you think?" So it sort of developed from there.

We ended up having an extra stage built for us at the Rainbow, because with two bands it would take far too long to strike each band's equipment and get everything else set up. Also, from the visual point of view they thought it was a good idea to have us on a stage above them.

OPPOSITE:
Sue, Dee Dee, Ruth,
Cherry and Babs
with Ian Anderson
of Jethro Tull
promoting 'The
Grand London
Return Concert'
outside the
Rainbow Theatre.

DEE DEE

The stage was enormous. We had to go up a ladder to get onto it. It was about the same size that we had on *Top of the Pops*, but there was nothing at the back or the sides in case we fell off. So it was rather terrifying dancing on top of this stage.

CHERRY

Flick made us wear these horrible and obscene costumes. The witch costume is the one I remember. It was all net, a sort of glittery, sequinny thing. The top half was all mesh, with sequins over our nipples, but from a distance it looked as if we were bare-breasted. I don't remember any of us being thrilled about this, but Flick thought it was hilarious at the time.

IAN ANDERSON

The costumes had mesh, and tinselly bits over the nipples. There wasn't even a hint of real flesh showing, but you could only tell that if you were standing six feet away. It was all very carefully calculated. I should know, I paid for it. "Holy shit Flick, you didn't tell me it was going to cost *that* much!" The girls were initially worried but soon entered into the spirit of things.

DEE DEE

We looked like glamorous witches, basically, with extremely long fingernails. An enormous contrast to the next number, for we just wore jeans and t-shirts in that. And then for the last number we wore togas.

We were wearing these diaphanous costumes and doing this very pretty pan pipe number that Ian had written. We were all in a big circle, and I had my back to the audience. Babs was opposite me and we were waving our arms around. Unfortunately, on one night Babs' shoulder-strap snapped and half her top fell down to her waist. She hadn't even realised, so I shrieked "Babs, your costume!" We weren't wearing bras, so the whole of the theatre got an eyeful of Babs' ample chest.

Cherry, Sue and Dee Dee dance to Barry White's 'You're the First, the Last, My Everything' on the 1974 Top of the Pops Christmas Special. *The group also performed the New Seekers' 'You Won't Find Another Fool Like Me' on the same show.*

Babs had to clasp her bosoms and dash off, which is very difficult when you're trying to shin down a ladder and preserve your dignity at the same time.

BABS

Just one strap went, and I exposed one boob. James Ramble, our ex-manager, was in the audience, and he was the only one that noticed. He went white. I thought, "Oh my gosh, what do I do?" I remember going off and the girls carrying on. Somebody gave me a safety pin and I joined them when I'd got myself safety-pinned up. The show must always go on!

IAN ANDERSON

We played for four nights and all had a very jolly time except for an escaping breast. There were several people backstage trying to stuff this escaped breast back where it belonged. But it was fun. They were a bunch of very nice girls who worked very hard.

Initially the audience were surprised – what are these interlopers doing here? The audience reacted in the same way as they would to a great goal-scorer from a team they didn't support themselves. But I think the girls got the feeling that they were well appreciated by the end.

SUE

One routine that always stands out for me was for the Christmas Day edition of *Top of the Pops* that year. It was the New Seekers' 'You Won't Find Another Fool Like Me' and we were these little fairies with red noses. It was done in two VTs, because Flick wanted the little fairies dancing around on the stage but she also wanted us up on trapezes.

DEE DEE

We did it dressed as clowns. They put us on trapezes, five or six feet off the floor, which doesn't seem very much, but when you're swinging from one it's pretty scary. Flick did have us doing some amazingly weird things.

SUE

Nobody told me about doing work without a safety net. You were hiked up above the floor, because Flick kept saying, "I don't want to see the set on the floor. I don't want to see it. Lift them higher. Higher!"

We were hanging on like grim death…

TEN
THE WRITING ON THE WALL
1975

★★★★★★★★★★★★★★★★★★★★★★★★★★★★★★★★★

DEE DEE

Right at the end of 1974 I became very ill, so for the first month or so of 1975 I wasn't functioning at all. I had some kind of virus that attacked my heart muscles.

Three days before Christmas I was taken into hospital. They thought I had meningitis and gave me a lumbar puncture. Two days later, feeling very groggy, I came out of hospital and went straight to my parents, where I recuperated for a couple of months.

Rod Stewart came to see me. We'd become friendly, Rod and I, at the end of 1974. Then unfortunately, just as we were about to go on our first date, I was taken ill. He did end up coming to the hospital. I was in St Mary's Hospital and was lying there like the Lady of the Camellias on her death bed, looking dreadful. A nurse came scuttling up to me, more excited than a rabbit with a carrot, and said, "Guess what, guess what? Rod Stewart's here!" And I thought, "Oh God, no."

And in he came, straight into the ward, fiddling with his hair as usual and carrying a large bunch of grapes. He then sat on my 'death' bed and held my hand. I didn't know whether to be happy, embarrassed or just squirm – but because I'd just had the lumbar puncture I couldn't move anyway.

He was very sweet and adorable. He came to visit me quite a few times at Parkside, which was this rather smart block of flats on Wimbledon Park

OPPOSITE:
Cherry and Dee Dee front a performance of Elton John's 'Island Girl' on Top of the Pops, *16 October 1975.*

Side where my parents lived. It was full of retired colonels and commanders. I remember looking out of the window one day and seeing Rod's enormous limousine arriving. All the curtains began twitching. All these strange colonels were peering through the windows, wondering "Who is *this* arriving at our establishment?"

CHERRY

Poor Dee Dee had all sorts of things wrong with her. She had a really bad spate of stuff. Her ankle, and a terrible and weird virus one time. I remember going over to Wimbledon to see her and seeing Rod Stewart. I was going in as Rod was coming out. He was keen on Dee Dee, I seem to remember.

DEE DEE

It took a while for me to recover so I became very depressed. I didn't really know what was the matter with me. As for the other girls… Status Quo's 'Down Down' was among the best numbers Pan's ever did; it was an iconic track and an incredible routine. But it was mid-January 1975 so I wasn't in it!

SUE

'Down Down' went down a storm. It was quite a raunchy number. Sadly, Dee Dee was ill that week so it was just Cherry, Babs, Ruth and myself.

Flick had these four podiums for us to stand on. Cherry was wearing a sexy suede skirt and off-the-shoulder top and looked a bit like Caroline Munro from the Lamb's Navy Rum ads. Babs' costume was a very pretty, flimsy chiffon dress revealing plenty of stockings and suspenders. Ruth had a Parisian look with split skirt and black fishnets, and I was dressed sort of Indian warrior style.

At rehearsals, you'd get people coming in to see what Pan's were doing that day, but that week the studio gradually filled up and up and up. I remember Robin Nash coming downstairs – he was a lovely man, famous for his bow ties and terribly loud laugh – and saying, "I think we'll run it

Filming a commercial for Woolworths.

just one more time, girls!"

We must have rehearsed it about four or five times… Something that didn't often happen with our other routines!

DEE DEE

One day, a friend of mine who worked for Epic Records – Louis Rodgers, brother of the pop star Clodagh Rodgers – came to see me and said, "Have a look at 'Miss Disc' 1975."

I opened the magazine and saw that people all around Britain had voted. I think Cherry was at number three and I was number five – out of all the girls in England! So that instantly made me feel better. It was just the tonic I needed. I rose out of my bed rather like Christ's resurrection; henceforth to my people… Back to wiggle my arse on the telly.

SUE

Another routine I particularly remember was for Barry White's 'What Am I Gonna Do With You', which all five of us did in March.

At *Top of the Pops* they used to have dry-ice machines – big cabinets that belched out smoke. And unfortunately they used to leave a wet residue on the floor. So you'd be slipping around, trying to dance. Flick had decided that, for this routine, we should have some kind of seaweed hanging down from the ceiling. So we were all being strangled with that. Plus there was a black PVC floor, so that was slippery. Plus the dry-ice machine was belching out all the smoke.

We were all dancing in line and following Babs down the side of the set. One minute I'm dancing behind Babs, the next minute she's gone. She's just disappeared. Completely. She'd fallen down somewhere. You couldn't see through the dry ice.

"Babs? Where are you? Where are you...?"

BABS

We had to dance through the audience and then each of us had to run up to the camera. When we rehearsed it, it was fine, but when we came to record it they turned on the dry ice. I ran into the audience, tripped over a camera cable, and then somebody tripped over me. And then I could hear a voice saying "Where's Babs?" I came up seeing stars.

DEE DEE

At the end of May we did the very first *Jim'll Fix It* show with a young girl called Vanessa Cullum, who was absolutely adorable. She must have been about eight. Vanessa's dream was to meet Pan's People and to dance with them. So on the show, you saw us meeting her and then her coming out in a little replica of our outfits and doing a dance with us to Slade's 'Thanks for the Memory'.

We'd had a lovely costume made for a number we did, 'Resurrection Shuffle' by Ashton, Gardner and Dyke... Long red and white striped

OPPOSITE:
Dancing with
young Vanessa
Cullum on Jim'll
Fix It, *31 May 1975.*

trousers – very very tight with a ruffle on the bottom – and green waistcoats. And Vanessa had exactly the same costume.

And then we sat down on a sofa and Jimmy gave her a *Jim'll Fix It* medal. She was really sweet and I really enjoyed meeting her. Funnily enough, I met her years later when I was dancing and choreographing, and she'd turned into a very good young dancer.

SUE

As well as opening shops and fêtes and lots of charity things, we'd even kick off football matches from time to time. We all signed autographs and Babs would get up and make a speech. Babs was always good at making speeches. And then we kicked off the match; I remember missing the ball.

Our chauffeur Ken had two lovely old Daimlers and, if it was feasible, he'd drive us to all these personal appearances. The rest of the time, if we had to travel further afield, it would be by train, often coming back on the sleeper at night.

On one occasion we finished a club gig in Leeds very late; we had to get back to rehearse *Top of the Pops*, and the midnight train to London was leaving in 20 minutes. There was no way we could change, so we ran down the platform at Leeds Station in pink beaded costumes and silver spray-on boots at nearly midnight, dashing past these completely stunned passengers. It must have made somebody's evening.

DEE DEE

About the same time, we performed in front of Princess Margaret at a big club up north. We didn't really want to do it because the next day we had a very early shoot in Aylesbury, but we agreed so long as we could go on early.

Unfortunately, Princess Margaret turned up late and then decided that she wanted to have a little go on the fruit machines. She always had a penchant for those. So we were in our dressing rooms waiting to perform and, finally, it was half past midnight when we went on. We came off and there was a message saying that the Princess would like to meet us. We declined and left. We weren't happy bunnies.

ROBERT POWELL

Pan's People first came to my attention, as they did with just about every other bloke in Britain, in the late 1960s. Every Thursday night, before we went out, me and my mate Dennis Waterman would watch *Top of the Pops* and I'd always say, "God, I fancy the blonde one."

Anyway… Cut to maybe six years later, when I happened to be at the BBC Club. I had a friend called Chris who was a floor manager on *Sports Night*, which went out on a Wednesday night, the same night that *Top of the Pops* was recorded. We were standing there at the bar when suddenly these five girls wandered in and parked themselves in a corner.

I looked at them and said, "Look over there, it's Pan's People.'

Chris said, "Yeah, they're in every Wednesday. Do you want to say hello to them?"

And I said "No, no, no! Of course I don't…"

He dragged me over and we sat down with the girls and chatted, which was very nice, and then they all went back to work. I rang him a couple of days later and said, "I think I might pop in again next Wednesday…"

So I went up the following Wednesday and I said to Chris, "I'm going to attempt something. I'm too shy to invite Babs out on her own, so I'm going to invite them all to dinner." So when the girls came in we bought them a drink and I said, "Would you like to come and have dinner after you've finished recording?" And amazingly these extraordinarily glamorous women all said yes.

So we went to a trattoria on the King's Road and had a great evening. I managed to sit next to Babs during dinner, and then we wrapped it up and I gave her a lift back to the BBC so she could pick up her MGB. And as I dropped her off at the BBC car park I said, "What are you doing at the weekend? Would you like to have dinner with me on Saturday night?"

And that was it really.

SUE

I can remember all the girls saying, "God. She's picked a really good-looking guy there." They had to keep it all very quiet and secret, which was virtually impossible. They managed for a while, which was nice.

DEE DEE

George Leventis was my childhood sweetheart when I lived in Africa. He was the son of a millionaire Greek businessman. We were engaged when I was 17. But when he threw my engagement ring from the window of our flat into the King's Road, I decided I wasn't going to marry him. I was too young anyway.

Then years later, just after Christmas 1974, I met him again. We started going out and he proposed to me, and I thought, "Well, why not?" It seemed like a good idea at the time. I shouldn't have been so stupid – I should've known that the second time around wasn't going to be any different. My parents were thrilled. My mother skipped over the moon and drank copious amounts of champagne. And then it all fell apart.

We started going out, but the trouble was he used to come with us on all the gigs. And he wouldn't leave me alone. He was so jealous; even if I went to the loo, he'd stand outside the door waiting for me. It got a bit out of hand after a while, and I think the girls got very fed up with George traipsing around after me. I handed in my notice to Pan's, saying that I was going to live on a Greek island which George was going to give me as a wedding present, but then after a few jealous bust-ups he threatened me with a gun and I had second thoughts.

So I escaped and hid at the home of Mike D'Abo from Manfred Mann. All the press showed up at Chelsea Registry Office on the 6th of June that year, and I wasn't there. My mother tore her hair out and retired to her bed for a week. But my father, in typical British fashion, said to me, "Oh never mind, old girl. As long as you're happy, I don't really care." And that was the end of it.

In the back of my mind, I suppose I was thinking that maybe I ought to

*Shredded jeans for a **Top of the Pops** number from 1975.*

settle down and get married, rather than cavort around and fall over all the time. I'd been in Pan's for almost nine years. The year before, my ankle had been really bad. Then I was sick at Christmas. And most of the time my ankle was strapped up. I suppose I liked the thought of the security of being married. I knew George very well. I knew his family. My parents would be thrilled. I'd have a family…

But it wasn't to be, and as quickly as I got into it I got out of it. George went back to Greece and married a beautiful Greek lady and I'm sure he's absolutely thrilled he didn't marry me. Because I was a bit of a liability, to be honest.

ROBERT POWELL

Babs and I didn't get any attention from the press at first. I remember that by the Christmas of '74 we'd been together for about three months, and I said, "Would you come and live with me?" So she moved in with me in

Babs marries Robert Powell in Goostrey, Cheshire, 29 August 1975.

the January of '75, and then of course the TV series *Jesus of Nazareth* came up and that was when the press got silly. It's hard to believe it now, but the very fact that we weren't married became an issue. Because I was suddenly playing Jesus of Nazareth, they went right through my life to see if they could get anything on me. The only thing they could dig up was that I was living with somebody to whom I wasn't married. So the people at *The Sun*, bless their cotton socks, decided that this would become an issue.

By now Babs and I had been together for well over six months, and this was a keeping relationship, we both knew that. And so I said, "Look, we're going to get married anyway, so why don't we just do it and shut them all up?"

We avoided the press by going to a very small church in a village called Goostrey in Cheshire, where one of my closest friends, the writer Alan Garner, lived. It was just Alan, his wife and child, my wife to be, the best man Mike King (of the King Brothers), Ken the Pan's People chauffeur who drove us up there, and our respective parents. That was it.

We did that on Friday the 29th of August 1975. Then we had lunch, drove back down to London, dropped Babs off at the flat, and then I continued to the Aldwych Theatre and went on stage.

BABS

The wedding happened very quickly. Robert proposed and two weeks later we were wed. We had to seek permission from the Archbishop of Canterbury, as we hoped to marry outside our diocese, and the permission came through only two days before the wedding. Because I didn't tell my parents till permission was granted, I didn't tell the girls either, feeling it was unfair to ask them to keep the secret.

We were married on a Friday. On the Saturday, Pan's went to Wales to do a gig and I took off my wedding ring. And the following day we hosted a little drinks party. The pretext was to say goodbye to Robert, who was about to go to north Africa to start filming *Jesus of Nazareth*.

And then, when everyone arrived, I said, "By the way girls, I know you'll probably be cross and upset with me for not telling you – but we're married."

DEE DEE

How she kept silent about it I don't know, but we were completely and utterly gobsmacked. We didn't know a thing.

And so there was Babs standing with Robert in their sitting room, with drinks and cheese on sticks, saying, "Hello, girls. Here's Robert, my husband. We got married on Friday. And he's going off to be *Jesus of Nazareth*, and I'm going with him."

End of story.

We all had our fans, but everybody remembered Babs. She was every man's dream; she was very sexy, with blonde hair and a sweet smile. I mean, Babs had everything going for her. The incredible thing about Babs was that she had no airs and graces. She wasn't arrogant, she was absolutely adorable; one of the nicest people you could ever meet in life.

BABS

I flew out to join Robert in Morocco, supposedly just for a two-week holiday, after which I'd go to and fro and maybe do a little freelance work if it came up. But that didn't happen. I arrived in Morocco and, as Robert puts it, he nailed my passport to the ceiling. So I was there for the duration.

When I met Robert I was 29, and I was 30 when we got married. I thought I didn't want him to take second place to Pan's People. So I decided at that point that I'd had a very good innings with the group and I'd achieved pretty well everything that was possible at that time to do. I felt I'd had an amazing time with Flick and the girls and now it was time to move on, hang up the dancing shoes and devote my life to Robert, having a family and being a housewife and a mum.

My last performance was on September the 18th – 'Feel Like Makin' Love' by Bad Company. It was quite an emotional time, really. It was closing the door on a particular era. It was tough.

For many weeks – months – afterwards, I had the feeling of missing something. Not just the camaraderie of the girls, but missing something that I couldn't quite put my finger on. Until it suddenly hit me one day that what I was missing was the adrenaline rush you get from actually performing. I remember Robert talking about it one day, and I suddenly thought, "Oh my gosh. That's it." It's like a drug.

ROBERT POWELL

We've been together ever since, and it's been an extraordinarily brilliant rollercoaster ride. The best thing I ever did was marrying my wife and having our kids. I can't think of anything I've done that's better.

DEE DEE

Babs leaving the group left an enormous void in Pan's. But we'd already started looking for new girls anyway, because I'd announced I was leaving after my engagement to George Leventis.

Actually we ended up with two new dancers, Lee Ward and Mary Corpe. At the end of the audition we were left with a few girls, and we really liked Mary and Flick really liked Lee. Lee was very dark, tall and

Summer 1975: in Sue's absence, Mary Corpe (centre) makes a cabaret appearance with the group while Babs (right) is still a member.

skinny. And Mary was sort of smaller, rounder, more like us – with long blonde hair. They first appeared on *Top of the Pops* with us on the 25th of September, dancing to Art Garfunkel's 'I Only Have Eyes for You'.

Mary was adorable. Amenable, warm, friendly; just a really nice girl. And very pretty too. Lee was a lovely dancer and a good-looking girl. So, on the screen, she fitted in beautifully. But behind the scenes, we met at rehearsals and that was it. No more to be said.

RUTH

In 1975 we did the Morecambe and Wise Christmas special. The whole world stopped to watch, didn't it? We were really honoured to be asked. I remember being quite daunted going into the rehearsal room. We weren't

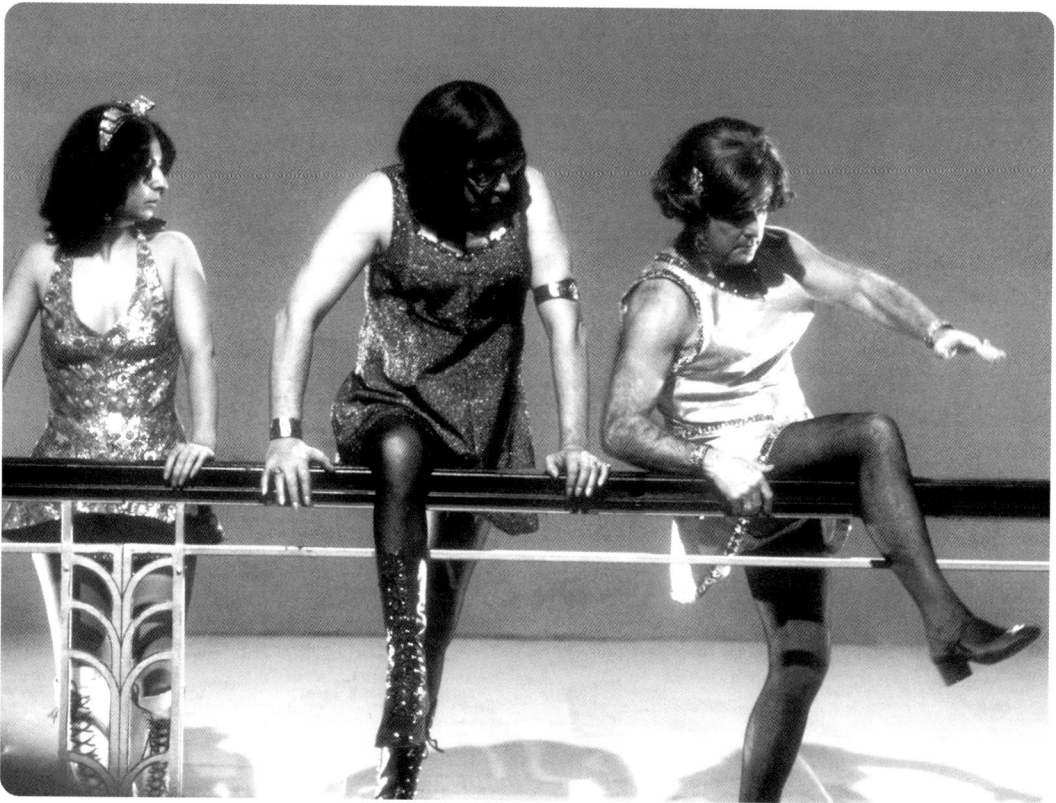

Ruth looks on as Ernie tries to get his leg over – performing 'Hey, Big Spender' on **The Morecambe and Wise Christmas Show.**

sure what to expect. They'd be sitting there, and it was very very serious.

Then we rehearsed together and they put me next to Eric. And, honestly, the only time I think I ever did that routine correctly was on the take in the studio. Because Eric just had me in hysterics the whole time. They worked really really hard. They were completely professional about it. It was just a joy to do.

SUE

They wanted us to do 'Hey, Big Spender'. The set was a ballet barre and in rehearsals we used to be weeping with laughter. Eric spent the whole time cracking jokes, and Ernie had problems actually getting his leg over the barre because he was so short. So he was taking a running jump at it.

CHERRY

Morecambe and Wise were off the scale. Oh, that was funny. The amount of jokes about 'getting your leg over' the barre. That was the trouble. We were howling with laughter. Howling.

But they had incredible discipline. It's well documented that they rehearsed and rehearsed and rehearsed; everything that looked off the cuff was really rehearsed. I think a lot of people thought it was just Eric, but it wasn't at all. Ernie was so clever and had a huge input into the whole thing. It was fascinating.

SUE

We didn't actually get to see them in costume until we taped the show. Even during rehearsals they hadn't come out in their costumes. And finally these two came out of the dressing room in make-up and mini-skirts.

Eric doesn't look good in a mini-skirt, but Ernie actually looked quite cute. They couldn't walk in their high heels. And I think we must have tried to take that routine two or three times because the camera crew were laughing, the floor manager was laughing, we were laughing. It was just ridiculous.

What a lovely pair to work for.

CHERRY

I was incredibly lucky because, years later, in 1983, they asked me to go and do a piece with them by myself. This was when they'd moved to ITV. They were doing a sort of mad gypsy encampment musical extravaganza, and I was playing the gypsy princess Eric was in love with. So I spent a couple of weeks with them and it was a complete joy.

Ernie told me on the quiet, "Eric gets really nervous around you."

"Why?" I asked.

"You have no idea," he replied, "but you are the spitting image of his first girlfriend. I remember when we were on tour together when we were 18 years old, and I cannot tell you – you are just the image of her."

And I said, "Oh, how lovely."

ABOVE:
Saying goodbye –
Dee Dee and Babs.

DEE DEE

I'd been off to Italy for a holiday, and while I was there I developed really bad hip trouble. My hip got better, but I felt that it was really time for me to hang up my boots.

I didn't want to leave, truth be told. Flick and I sat down and had a chat about it. I think she felt it was time for me to go as well, because I was so injured by that time. The only reason I hadn't left already was because being in Pan's offered so much security. So it was time for me to say goodbye, basically, and I bowed out of Pan's People in November.

And that was the end of me. It was a very sad – and terrifying – moment. From being in Pan's and having found fame and some degree of financial security, I was suddenly on my own and out on a limb.

I was 29 years of age. And I had no idea of what I was going to do.

OPPOSITE:
The new line-up –
Ruth, Mary, Lee,
Sue and Cherry –
dance to David
Bowie's 'Space
Oddity' on the 1975
Top of the Pops
Christmas Special.

ELEVEN
CURTAIN CALL
1976-79

★★★★★★★★★★★★★★★★★★★★★★★★★★★★★★★★★★★★★★★

SUE

In February 1976, *Blue Peter*'s Lesley Judd joined us for a week. She'd been asked, as an item for *Blue Peter*, to spend a week with Pan's People and learn a routine for *Top of the Pops*. She was a former dancer anyway; ten years earlier she'd been one of The Beat Girls, and she'd also worked with The Young Generation.

So she came in for rehearsals in the seedy gymnasium we used. They used to play bingo next door, so from week to week we'd hear the old biddies going "Number nine!" as we rehearsed. The *Blue Peter* crew came down and filmed us, and Lesley ended up actually appearing on the show dancing to a Spanish thing with us – 'Rodrigo's Guitar' by Manuel and the Music of the Mountains. Noel Edmonds was the presenter and said, "It doesn't take a brilliant mathematician to realise that Pan's People have grown in number…"

She was good. She said she'd found it quite difficult, but having been an ex-dancer I don't think she was all that fazed.

CHERRY

By 1976, though, Babs and Dee Dee had both left and it really wasn't Pan's People for me. Each girl had been so well known individually that it became more and more difficult to replace them. It's a different thing if it's five dancers you don't know; it isn't a big deal. That's why it all had to come to an end.

OPPOSITE:
Dee Dee marries Captain Andrew Corbet Burcher at the Royal Artillery military barracks in Woolwich, 18 December 1978.

SUE

Within three months of each other, Babs and Dee Dee both left. So by the end of 1975 the line-up was Ruth, Cherry, myself, Mary and Lee.

Mary Corpe and Lee Ward were both very good dancers and very nice girls. But it wasn't the original Pan's People. And I think the fans were disappointed to see their favourites disappearing – Babs going, Dee Dee going. Being given the opportunity to replace Louise had been a biggie, because I remember thinking at the time, "How can I replace this girl? She was one of the originals."

So as the originals started to leave, it became apparent to Flick, Ruth, Cherry and myself that things were going to change. You can't keep remodelling the same old thing; sometimes it's best just to start something new, which is what happened.

RUTH

Flick and I thought that Pan's had run its course. It was time for somebody else to have a shot. I think we slightly overstayed our welcome. The last six months, anyway.

When Mary and Lee joined, it was clear that it wasn't really working. It was just a bit old hat; it needed a new format. Flick and I had discussed it even before Babs and Dee Dee left, when I offered to be the first one to leave. But I ended up being the last one! We wanted to form another group, with boys in it – which became Ruby Flipper.

SUE

Ruth had already decided that she didn't necessarily want to carry on dancing. And Flick, I think, wanted to do something different. And that was when she decided to start a mixed group. At the beginning of the year she and Ruth had decided that Ruth was going to move from being a dancer into management. That's when Ruth and Flick formed Ruby Flipper Ltd, which was the management company. And out of that came the very short-lived Ruby Flipper group.

I remember Cherry and I were talking with Ruth and Flick, and they said, "This is what's going to happen. We want to do something different, but we don't want to go public with it yet." Because when they started Ruby Flipper, it was done originally without the BBC's knowledge. It was something Ruth and Flick wanted to build up and then present to the BBC as a replacement for Pan's.

RUTH

The last Pan's performance was very sad.

It was the 29th of April and we did two numbers. The Four Seasons' 'Silver Star' was one of them, and we had these star-shaped silver crowns on our heads. I remember mine falling down my face, so I didn't look very elegant. But it was very moving for me, thinking it was the last time I was going to dance. I was just hoping I would get it right, and thinking, "Gosh, is this going to be the last time?"

It was sad. The end of an era.

Sue in star-spangled pants dancing to 'Midnight Rider' by Paul Davidson on Top of the Pops, 22 January 1976.

SUE

Ruth got a long goodbye solo in the middle of 'Silver Star', which was

lovely. I think she must have been nearly in tears doing that. After doing it for so many years, and then hanging up your hoofing boots – your silver spray-on boots. And that was that.

CHERRY

By then, for me, Pan's People wasn't really Pan's People any more. So it would've had more resonance had we all – the original group – stopped at one particular point. I think that would've been much more poignant. Instead we were just rehearsing the next show, as Ruby Flipper.

SUE

Ruby Flipper started rehearsing towards the end of Pan's People. And that was awkward sometimes, because Flick hadn't invited all of us to join the new group. Cherry and I had to do rehearsals without Mary and Lee being there.

RUTH

Robin Nash knew all about Ruby Flipper and was well up for it. But when Bill Cotton found out he was furious. He was in charge of Light Entertainment at the time and hauled us both in, Flick and me. He said he wasn't happy because one of the guys was black and was dancing with white girls. Of course, we found this attitude horrifying. But he said he wanted another girl group; either we went ahead with that or we lost the gig – we'd be out. So we didn't have a choice.

SUE

You can't hide things from a big corporation like that. When you're phasing out an all-girl group and bringing in something so radically different, you do need to tell people. Perhaps Flick thought, "If I tell them this, they're going to say no." Well, she was right!

But I think even an all-girl group would have had a tough time following Pan's People. People would have said, "It's not the same." Pan's People were the first.

CHERRY

Ruby Flipper wasn't what I wanted to do. I watched some of it recently and it wasn't very good at all. It didn't have the tongue-in-cheek nonsense that Pan's People had about it. Ruby Flipper just wasn't good enough really. Looking back, I probably would've preferred to have left with Pan's People.

I had the chance to audition for a show called *A Chorus Line*, a big American musical that was coming in to the West End. The Radio 1 DJ Annie Nightingale had taken me to see it. I didn't know Annie terribly well, but we were in the same kind of gang socially; her husband, Binky Baker, couldn't make it so she asked me to go in his place. And I suppose it was about ten minutes in when the tears started rolling down my face.

Ruby Flipper are introduced to the press, 6 May 1976: (left to right) Cherry Gillespie, Floyd Pearce, Patti Hammond, Philip Haigh, Lulu Cartwright, Gavin Trace and Sue Menhenick.

197

I was watching the show and thinking, "Finally, this is it. This is what I should be doing. This is what I was trained to do."

And that kind of prompted me to leave, so I gave in my notice for Ruby Flipper. I got the job in *A Chorus Line* and it was absolutely wonderful. It was at the Theatre Royal Drury Lane and I was in it for two years. It was without doubt the highlight of my career. It was just amazing.

And all thanks to Annie Nightingale. And to Binky for not wanting to go!

RUTH

After six months we disbanded Ruby Flipper and put together another girl group, which Flick and I held auditions for. That's how Legs & Co was formed.

SUE

Ruby Flipper was given the chop, and I don't think Flick had any choice in the matter. The BBC wanted more control over it. They decided that there was going to be a new *Top of the Pops* dance group and – very cleverly – they gave viewers the opportunity to decide on the name. So it was very much a dance group that was created by the BBC.

Ruth and Flick managed Legs & Co but we were contracted by the BBC, so it was more restricted. Legs & Co started in 1976 and ran through to 1981. We were popular, but in a completely different way. Not in the iconic way that Pan's People were.

Sadly, it was in the late 1970s and early '80s that we started to be given more of the novelty records. Pan's People had done some funny numbers as well, like 'The Monster Mash'. But they never had to dress up as a Smurf or do 'The Birdie Song'. One week you'd be wearing a Diana Ross gown with a big fur and beautiful diamond ear-rings; the next you'd be a Smurf. Get the blue paint on and the glasses and the white beard, and you were away.

DEE DEE

When I left Pan's People, I didn't really know what to do. I was so lost.

Pan's stopped in May 1976, about six months after I'd left, and towards the end of that year I formed the New Pan's People. The problem was that a lot of the newspapers just called them Pan's People. I think it must have been quite jarring for the girls to open up their papers and see the New Pan's People. In hindsight, I wish now I hadn't done it. But you do things you regret and you just move on.

We went around the country doing loads of cabaret. We were once thrown out of Bahrain by the Ayatollah after having a picture taken in front of a mosque.

In 1975 I'd become one of the founder members of the Nordoff-Robbins Charity for autistic children, which became the biggest rock charity in the world. They have an event every year called the Silver Clef Awards, which was my idea. I was very involved in the beginning, doing all the advertising and getting money in from the big record companies.

During the late '70s I worked with Benny Hill as his choreographer for a few years. He could be quite difficult because he was such a perfectionist, but he was also kind and considerate to me and my dancers. I stopped working for him when my son Alex was born in December 1979.

CHERRY

After Pan's People, the person that I was always in touch with was Flick. I'd speak to the other girls on the phone sometimes. And it's always great seeing everybody.

It was a very small part of my life – 1972 to 1976. It was only about four years, but it was an incredibly intense four years. So much happened.

EPILOGUE
POST PAN'S

★★★★★★★★★★★★★★★★★★★★★★★★★★★★★★★★★★★★★

RUTH

When Legs & Co finished on *Top of the Pops*, Flick and I carried on with a dance troupe called Zoo.

Zoo wasn't a group as such, it was just a name. Flick used to hire different dancers for whatever was needed. They'd be in the audience or they might do a little number. Flick continued to do the choreography while I did the business side.

I hated it, to be honest, but did my best.

SUE

After we stopped doing *Top of the Pops* in 1981, Legs & Co did a few more bits of television. We did a lot of cabaret, travelling around. We did the Middle East; we did Cairo, Bahrain, Dubai, Abu Dhabi. We did some German television and we did a tour of Ireland for a couple of weeks. Then in 1983 we decided enough was enough.

CHERRY

Having finished in *A Chorus Line*, I decided to go back to my roots, back into drama. So I did a lot of theatre. I was also lucky to get the odd series on TV and a little part, Midge, in the Bond film *Octopussy*, which was a

OPPOSITE:
Babs at the magnetic North Pole having just completed the first Polar Race, 2003.

fantastic experience.

Then I did two series of *The Hot Shoe Show* with Wayne Sleep for the BBC. We were a company of dancers gathered from various shows in the West End. We sang, had guest choreographers, performed skits and all sorts of things. Then I went back into the theatre and played Jane Bennet in *Pride and Prejudice* at the Old Vic. I was very lucky to have such a varied career.

DEE DEE

Around 1981 my then-husband and I decided to try our hand at producing West End shows and put on something called *The Mad Show* – which, unfortunately, was a huge flop. Because we'd put a lot of our own money into it, we lost our house.

That didn't deter us, and we produced another show called *Le Cirque Imaginaire*, starring Victoria Chaplin, daughter of Charlie Chaplin, and her husband Jean-Baptiste Thierrée. Luckily this one was a huge hit and helped recoup some of the money we lost on the first show.

About that time I had the idea of starting my own dance club. I found a little studio in a building that belonged to Roger Waters of Pink Floyd. It was at the top of the building so I called it the Dance Attic. I taught four classes in the morning and four classes in the evening, and the studio began to get a bit too busy. We moved into a much larger building in Putney Bridge Road, then to the old Fulham Baths in Fulham Broadway.

And Dance Attic just got bigger and bigger. Everyone from Tommy Steele to Ian McKellen to Take That have been through the Dance Attic's doors.

SUE

When Legs & Co folded, I started working more as a freelance dancer. I ended up doing some work with Mick Karn, the bassist in the band Japan, and then worked on the Monty Python film *The Meaning of Life*. I was one of the angels in heaven, flying up and down with wings on. Then I decided I wanted to start a family. I thought, "I've done my selfish bit for a while, now it's time to try being a mum."

RUTH

When Zoo finished in 1982, I finished too.

After that I didn't want anything to do with showbusiness. But I didn't really know what to do with myself. I'd always loved cooking so I thought I'd like to get into the catering trade. I went to work at a fish restaurant in Richmond for six months. It was a wonderful experience, but I'd never worked so hard in all my life.

So I thought maybe I should teach fitness classes. There was something at the time called Trim Tone, which evolved from the Canadian army and was keep-fit mixed with yoga. So I did that for a few years and taught at Dee Dee's studio. But I was getting older and teaching keep-fit isn't really a long-term career.

So eventually I just decided it was time I learnt to type and use a computer. I did a course and then I temped for about ten years, and eventually got a job with Hammersmith and Fulham Council, which I loved. I was very proud of what I achieved there, because it didn't come naturally. I did quite well in the end, and met some wonderful people that I'm still friends with today.

CHERRY

Nowadays I do charity work for dancers. I'm on the board of something called Dancers Career Development. When dancers get to the magical age of 35, their bodies just say, "You know what? I really think that's enough." Everything just gets more difficult, more painful, and so dancers have to reinvent themselves.

But unlike footballers, who likewise have very limited careers, dancers don't get paid in the same way and have no savings. So Dancers Career Development administers a very small fund, meaning people can apply for grants to re-train in anything they want to do. We help as much as we can, but we never have enough money.

Dee Dee and husband Henry Marsh with family.

DEE DEE

I'm now married to Henry Marsh, whom I first met back in 1974 at the record company convention in Eastbourne. He still rocks with his band Sailor, as well as mentoring young musical protégées. I'm still dancing down in the West Country, where we live, and I have my own dance club. Teaching others what I've been doing all my life is hugely rewarding.

ROBERT POWELL

Babs did this extraordinarily old-fashioned thing. When she was 30 she married me, stopped dancing and spent the next 20 years completely devoted to running me and the children and the house. But when she hit 50, she looked around and saw that the kids didn't really need her any more. So she suddenly decided that she'd run the Marathon – never having run more than ten yards in her life.

She ran it, then announced that she was going to apply to sail around the world – never having been on a yacht in her life. I was convinced she'd never get a berth; it was just impossible to sail for a year in the worst oceans in the world. But she got the berth.

Everybody thought she would drop out. They had a sweepstake on the boat, and they all thought she would be the first to go. But when they finished the ten months at sea her skipper said that, if he was to do the whole thing over again, she'd be the first person he'd ask to join his crew. Not because she was the greatest sailor, because she wasn't. But she was just the greatest person to have on board.

BABS

I loved the days at sea. I never got bored. We went round Cape Horn and then our young skipper, Will Carnegie, had a call on the satellite phone from London, asking if I could do a magazine interview. So I sat at the navigation table, miles from anywhere, deep in the Southern Ocean, and talked to this young girl back in London.

It seemed so surreal. She said, "You used to be a dancer, and now you're sailing. That's very different, isn't it?"

And I said, "Actually, there's a great similarity between the disciplines of what I did with Pan's People and what I'm doing now. What I've had to do is bring those disciplines back into play. They're just different tools. Then it was the discipline of dancing, now it's sailing discipline. The only difference being that sailing is life-threatening, so team work is even more crucial."

The discipline of 'the show must go on' is absolutely true. That's the most important thing. And so when it came to sailing, I never missed a watch. I could never call myself a sailor as such, but what was important was to find my place in the team and learn what I could contribute. I learnt how to stitch sails, badly. I learnt how to make a good cuppa for my watch leader and skipper Will. And I got a reputation for smuggling the occasional illicit bottle of bubbles on board. A girl should never travel without her little black dress, some stilettos and a bottle of bubbles!

I came back after ten months having realised that there could be many adventures outside the home and family. So as and when opportunities arose, I said yes instead of no. And doing that has taken me to all sorts of fascinating, obscure and remote places, and also given me the chance to meet some remarkable people. And by taking part in these treks and adventures, many wonderful people have helped me raise money for various charities.

ROBERT POWELL

Babs has no concept of the word 'can't'. Since then she's done Everest base camp, she's done the jungle in Guyana, she's done Iceland, she's done the Sahara, she's done Kilimanjaro, she's done Nepal, she's sailed around the world, she's done the North Pole and the South Pole. Now that's not bad for an ex-hoofer, is it?

PAUL SMITH

By 1994 I'd left the BBC and was running the independent production company Celador. To mark the 30th anniversary of *Top of the Pops*, we came up with the idea of doing a television documentary about Pan's People.

We'd managed to track down a videotape editor who had some old *Top of the Pops* recordings. At the BBC they used to have what was called a wipe order, which would come down from the unit manager of each department – to erase videotapes. The then-policy was that material that was no longer required would be erased, because the value of the videotape was more important than what had been recorded on it. That's why masses of wonderful television was lost forever.

But there was a videotape editor who, when the orders came in, copied off the Pan's People routines before the actual tapes were erased. He stuffed them on an end bit of tape and stored them away under his bed. So the inspiration to make the documentary came about because we discovered this guy. He was terrified that the BBC would take action against him, so we had to get an undertaking from the BBC that they wouldn't sue him if it was admitted he was the source of the material.

The programme, which we called *Digging the Dancing Queens*, was commissioned just a month before broadcast! We put the show together, researched it, shot it and edited it in a few days.

BABS

It was so nice of Paul to get us all together. We reminisced about the old days and took a trip down memory lane. And there was a wonderful response to it. We were thrilled.

PAUL SMITH

It was just a piece of simple entertainment that chronicled the success of Pan's People and reminded viewers just how phenomenally huge they were. The documentary was tremendously well received; it's been repeated three times.

FUNNY, INTELLIGENT, 100% ACRYLIC   4TH AUGUST 1989   £1 - US $2.95

PUNCH

Babs? Cherry?
Thingybob?
That Blonde One...

WHAT HAPPENED TO PAN'S PEOPLE?

PLUS
ALLAN BORDER PRAISED
CLUB X TERMINATED
AND
HAROLD PINTER DISINTERRED

Pan's People are featured in **Punch** *magazine, 4 August 1989.*

BABS

Flick went on and choreographed musicals. But I think she was torn between her need to be here and her desire to go back to America. And I think, ultimately, she decided that the pull to go home was greater than her wish to be here.

She died in May 2011, aged only 65. Flick put up an incredible fight against cancer. She battled with it for 24 years. She was inspiring in her battle. She never complained, she never let it get her down, she never allowed it to interfere with her life. It was just part and parcel of things. She would have her treatments and not let it stop her coming over to visit us, or us going to visit her in the States.

We knew that she was very ill, and it got to a point where it was just a matter of time. We wanted to go over to be with Flick but I don't think she wanted us to see her in those latter days. She wanted us to remember her in the fullness of life.

Flick didn't want a funeral as such, so she went to the hospital and then went to dust. There was no service. But what she'd done in her last days was choreograph her own memorial celebration.

It was magical. It was at the house which she had built herself, just outside Clinton in upstate New York, in the middle of cornfields and woods. It was a beautiful place, a beautiful house. Ruth, Dee Dee, Louise and I all flew over, and Cherry joined us. The sun shone, the weather was glorious. I suppose it was her last act of choreography.

DEE DEE

It was a beautiful sunny day. We went up to a small gazebo where Flick's cousin scattered her ashes.

While that was happening, the one thing I remember was the butterfly. A butterfly rested on the gazebo, and then flew all the way around it and then down towards the ashes and fluttered around there. And then it disappeared. I thought, "Oh my God, that's Flick."

BABS

Nigel Lythgoe, the choreographer, came to her memorial service too. He phoned up and asked if he could join the team, and we said of course you can, we'd be honoured if you were there. He said he found Flick an inspiration when he was a young dancer – her creativity and her fearlessness in breaking new ground.

Flick wasn't afraid. She wasn't afraid to do something serious and she wasn't afraid to do something silly, or zany, or raunchy, or balletic. She was extraordinary because she was breaking new ground all the time, always innovating. I think Flick could turn her hand to anything.

CHERRY

I absolutely adored Flick, and I miss her terribly. I think I was lucky. I was out of it all by 21, and I then went on to have my career, if you like. I just wish Flick could have gone on to do more, because there was so much more she could have done. She was very confined by *Top of the Pops*.

SUE

Flick was great to work with.

She was one of those people who was always one step ahead. I saw the way she developed as a choreographer, how she managed the transition between three groups (Pan's People, Ruby Flipper and Legs & Co), and how she interpreted all the music that came out over those years. She was a very clever lady. For someone to keep coming up with a routine every single week of the year… I don't know how she did it. And I don't think there's ever been a choreographer that's done it, before or since.

I learnt a lot from her. I owe an enormous amount to her patience and to the experience she gave me.

BABS

Flick I absolutely adored. We all adored her, because she was intelligent, funny, feisty, loyal, kind, creative, witty, unafraid. And she faced her illnesses with such strength and fortitude.

When Flick went, I felt like I'd lost a limb. I still do. When you hung up the phone after a conversation with Flick, you felt you'd learnt something. You felt that you could face the world again. You just longed for her next visit to the UK so that you could have fun together, so you could hang out together. She found the funky restaurants, she knew where to shop, she knew what places and shows and art galleries she wanted to go and see.

She was a very wise woman, and a very brave woman. She was one of the most inspiring women I've ever met.

RUTH

We were kind of warned with Flick. We were prepared. We were not prepared for Louise.

BABS

Louise's husband Tony died in 2010. After that – well, Lulu and Tony had been such an inseparable couple she found it very difficult living without him. Her stepson Anthony and daughter-in-law Helen moved her to Suffolk, where she'd be close to them, and she seemed happy enough for a while.

Then one day Helen went to visit her and she didn't answer the door. Louise had collapsed, so Helen and Anthony rushed her to hospital and called me. They said it was serious, but suggested I wait till she'd seen her specialist before visiting. But by lunchtime the next day Louise had died. Her heart simply stopped. Anthony and Helen, and her dear son Tony, were with her.

I think she died of a broken heart. It was tragic; she was only 63.

DEE DEE

Babs rang me and I burst into tears. Ruthie was trying to calm me down. I think it's difficult for people to understand what an incredible bond we girls had, and still have all these years later. Losing Flick was bad enough, but then to lose Louise…

BABS

Louise's stepson organised the most wonderful funeral in Woodbridge, Suffolk. Cherry came from France, Dee Dee came to my house and Robert drove us there. It was a very beautiful occasion but very sad, very poignant.

DEE DEE

We walked into church and down the aisle, all of us Pan's together, and everyone's eyes were on us. I remember thinking that I mustn't cry, and then they played 'Little Child (Daddy Dear)' by Wes Montgomery. It was the number we did on the *In Concert* special, and I couldn't stop the tears. They came tumbling down.

Louise was the most gorgeous, sexy, sultry, beautiful woman. And she didn't suffer fools gladly. I would say, out of us all, she was the toughest.

CHERRY

Louise was lovely, absolutely lovely. I was incredibly fond of her. I also thought she was extremely beautiful. Her body was beautiful; her face was exquisite. And she was very funny. And she made the best egg mayonnaise sandwiches. She wasn't necessarily a cook, but my God she made fantastic egg mayonnaise sandwiches.

BABS

I loved Louise. Not a day goes by when I don't miss her. She became a very good friend. She was a kind person, very open-hearted. I don't remember anything ever being too much trouble for her. She was a wonderful, uplifting person. We could banter for hours about nonsense, really. She was a very dear, very loyal friend.

★ ★ ★ ★ ★ ★

RUTH

I think most of us who were young in the 1960s and '70s would say how lucky we were, especially to be in the business we were in. How lucky to be successful and earning our living by dancing. You couldn't wish for anything better. We worked hard, but that doesn't matter when you're doing what you want to do, what you've dreamed of since you were a little girl. How many people can say that?

DEE DEE

I'd always wanted to be a dancer, and I achieved that. And I achieved it in one of the most iconic dance groups in England. I think Pan's will go down in history because we were the first.

RUTH

Yes, we were the first of our kind. I think we opened the door for a lot of the dancing that we see today. And for better or worse, we were in control; we ran our own business affairs. Which for a group of young girls then was unheard of.

BABS

Pan's People was an innovative group for its time. It was new, it hadn't been done, and it was great to be part of something that was breaking new ground. Dare I say it, it was perhaps the forerunner of dance as we know it today. I'm really proud of our legacy. And it's lovely to be remembered all these years on.

SUE

I learnt so much during my early days with Pan's People. Pan's People was, for me, the beginning of being able to do a job that I loved doing. And how many people can say that? It was fantastic.

CHERRY

I just don't know what it was – whether it was the period, the fashion connection, the music, the party element of the 1970s. I have no idea. But something happened at that point with Pan's People, for sure. It was a magic of some kind.

We definitely had no idea of the impact *Top of the Pops* had. I had my hair cut short about five years ago, but until then I was still recognised everywhere. Thirty-five years later people still remembered. I found that amazing – the power of TV.

DEE DEE

My memories are of all the wonderful dances Flick choreographed, the amazing costumes, and the incredible camaraderie and friendship.

RUTH

I remember rehearsals and things going wrong. I remember Babs falling over and all the hysterical laughter. I remember meeting Jack Jones for the first time with smut all over our faces because we were freezing cold; all the weird, unglamorous stuff. We had the time of our life.

BABS

With Pan's People, what has endured are the friendships. Through the decades we've stayed close. Time and distance have sometimes separated us but we've always come together. I have the most wonderful memories. We followed our dreams.

It was the most wonderful decade of my life.

CHRONOLOGY

1945

28 November: Barbara (Babs) Lord born – Wolverhampton, Staffordshire

1946

23 March: Felicity (Flick) Colby born – Hazelton, Pennsylvania

13 July: Ruth Pearson born – Kingston, Surrey

24 September: Patricia (Dee Dee) Wilde born – Farnham, Surrey

1947

8 August: Andrea (Andi) Rutherford born – London

1949

3 September: Louise Clarke born – London

1955

7 February: Cherry Gillespie born – Hemsby, Norfolk

9 September: Sue Menhenick born – Benghazi, Libya

1964

6 July: first episode of *The Beat Room* (BBC2) with resident dancers The Beat
   Girls (featuring Ruth and Babs)

1965

1 February: *The Beat Room* is renamed *Gadzooks! It's All Happening* and runs until
   27 September

1966

Unknown date: Ruth forms separate group, Tomorrow's People

Unknown date: Flick joins The Beat Girls

7 May: Dee Dee joins The Beat Girls

9 July: first appearance by The Beat Girls on *The Dickie Valentine Show* (ITV)

31 August: The Beat Girls (Dee Dee, Babs, Flick, Lorelly Harris, Penny Fergusson, Diane South) go to the Venice Film Festival to promote *Fahrenheit 451*

8 December: Pan's People formed by Flick, Dee Dee and Babs; Lorelly and Penny also recruited, plus Felicity Balfour

21 December: first Pan's People performance (Babs and Lorelly), Liège

1967

8 January: first monthly appearance on *Vibrato* (RTB, Belgium) [continuing into 1968-69]

March: Felicity leaves, Ruth joins

14 May: opening night of *Gulliver* (Belgian National Opera / Béjart Ballet Company, Brussels)

June: appearance on *Carousel d'Été* (RTB-BRT, Belgium)

11 August: first appearance (of seven) on *The Dickie Valentine Show* (ITV)

26 August: appearance at the Gouden Zeezwaluw festival – Knokke, Belgium

December: Penny leaves, Louise joins

22 December: to Zurich for *Hits a Go-Go* (SBC, Switzerland)

also: *Beat Club* (Bremen Radio-TV, Germany) and *Moef GaGa* (VARA, Holland)

1968

9 February: opening night of *Die Fledermaus* (Belgian National Opera / Béjart Ballet Company, Brussels)

16 February: first appearance on *Beat Beat Beat* (Hessischer Rundfunk, Germany)

March: Lorelly leaves, Andi joins

4 April: Dee Dee and Ruth (with The Gojos) appear on *Top of the Pops* (BBC1) ['Simon Says' by The 1910 Fruitgum Company]

17 April: Lorelly departs for Paris

18 April: first Pan's People performance (Dee Dee, Ruth, Flick) on *Top of the Pops* ['Cry Like a Baby' by The Box Tops]

30 May: first full group Pan's People performance on *Top of the Pops* ['US Male' by Elvis Presley]

13 July: first appearance (of six) on *Bobbie Gentry* (BBC2)

12 October: first confirmed appearance on *Beat Club* (Bremen Radio-TV, Germany)

24 November: first appearance (of four) on *Herman van Veenshow* (VARA, Holland)

28 December: first appearance (of 13) on *Happening for Lulu* (BBC1)

also: *The Golden Shot* (ITV), *Top of the Night* (RTE, Eire) and *Go-Go Gig* (RTB-BRT, Belgium)

OPPOSITE:
Posing with Dutch cyclist Jan Janssen at the National Stadium of Madrid in 1967. The following year, Janssen would become the first Dutchman to win the Tour de France.

Pan's People Our Story

OPPOSITE:
***With members of
the crew of HMS
Eagle during the
group's visit to
Malta, May 1971.***

1969

17 May: appearance on *Des O'Connor On Stage* (ITV)

25 May: appearance on *Jean Ferrat* (VARA, Holland)

18 June: first appearance (of 12) on *Bobbie Gentry* series two (BBC2)

9 August: first appearance on *The Frankie Howerd Show* (ITV)
[note: Penny replaced Ruth in this six-part series]

9 September: first of four episodes of *Decidedly Dusty* (BBC1) [choreographer: Ruth]

9 November: appearance in documentary *London Aktuell* (ZDF, Germany)

20 November: first appearance (of three) on *The Price of Fame or Fame at Any Price* (BBC2)

24 December: broadcast of *With a Little Help from My Friends* (ITV)

25 December: appearance on *The Price of Fame* Christmas special (BBC2)

1970

7 January: Louise hailed as 'Top of the Poppets' in the *Daily Mirror*

23 April: to Brize Norton for *Top of the Pops* filming with the Royal Marines

14 October: opening of *Lie Down, I Think I Love You* at the Strand Theatre, with Louise in the cast; it closes after 13 performances

1971

1 February: first appearance (of six) on *Gentry* (BBC2)

16 April: recording of *Toppop: Golden Earring Special* (VARA, Holland)

May: filming for *Top of the Pops* with the Royal Navy in Malta

May: performing at the *Daily Mirror* Hot Pants Ball, Lyceum Theatre London

5 June: first appearance on *Disco 71* (ZDF, Germany)

July: second appearance at the Gouden Zeezwaluw festival – Knokke, Belgium

December: to Mombasa for *Top of the Pops* filming with the Royal Navy

1972

April: Flick quits as a Pan's People dancer but continues as choreographer

30 April: broadcast of *Nancy Wilson from the Talk of the Town* (BBC2)

7 May: broadcast of *Glen Campbell from the Talk of the Town* (BBC2)

27 July / 3 August: appearances on *Nationwide* (BBC1)

17 August: appearance on *Night Club* (BBC1)

October: Andi leaves

December: filming with Frankie Howerd in Northern Ireland

28 December: Cherry's debut on *Top of the Pops* ['Without You' by Nilsson]

1973

20 January: appearance on *Cilla* (BBC1)

14 March: broadcast of *Frankie Howerd in Ulster* (BBC1)

29 April: first appearance (of six) on *The John Denver Show* (BBC2)

15 September: Pan's People hailed as 'sex symbols of the generation' in *Record Mirror*

27 September: first appearance (of eight) on *Show of the Week: The Two Ronnies* (BBC1)

31 December: *In Concert* recorded

1974

20 January: first appearance (of four) on *The Jack Jones Show* (BBC2)

16 February: appearance on *Clunk-Click* (BBC1)

17 April: broadcast of *In Concert* (BBC2)

May: Louise leaves, Sue joins

6 June: Sue's debut on *Top of the Pops*

9 August: release of first Pan's People single, 'You Can Really Rock and Roll Me'

14-17 November: Rainbow Theatre residency with Jethro Tull

24 December: appearance on *Crackerjack: Aladdin* (BBC1)

1975

30 May: release of second Pan's People single, 'He's Got Magic'

31 May: appearance on *Jim'll Fix It* (BBC1)

4 July: release of Mike McGear single 'Dance the DO', with Pan's People on the sleeve

September: Babs leaves

25 September: debut of Mary Corpe and Lee Ward on *Top of the Pops*

November: Dee Dee leaves

December: appearance at the Hammersmith Odeon with Slade

25 December: appearance on *The Morecambe and Wise Christmas Show* (BBC1)

1976

16 February: appearance with Lesley Judd on *Blue Peter* (BBC1)

1 April: Lee leaves [her last *Top of the Pops* performance is on this date]

29 April: final Pan's People appearance on *Top of the Pops*
    ['More, More, More' by Andrea True Connection plus 'Silver Star' by
    The Four Seasons]

ACKNOWLEDGEMENTS

★★★★★★★★★★★★★★★★★★★★★★★★★★★★★★★★★★★★

Babs, Cherry, Dee Dee and Ruth would like to thank...

Stanley Dorfman, without whom…

Our great supporter and friend Jonathan Wood, and Tessa Watts-Russell – our choreologist and Pan's People dogsbody!

James Ramble, our manager; our agents, Peter Prichard and Dick Katz; and our publicist Philip Day.

Nigel Lythgoe, for paying tribute to Flick in his excellent foreword.

The director-producers of *Top of the Pops*: Stan Appel, Michael Hurll, Johnnie Stewart, Robin Nash, Colin Charman, Mel Cornish and musical director Johnnie Pearson.

So many of the behind-the-scenes staff – the camera operators, sound and lighting technicians, vision mixers and PAs, especially Gill Stribling-Wright and Kate Greer. Also the costume designers and wardrobe departments that collaborated with Flick, in particular Mary Husband.

The guys on the BBC gates, who gave us the best parking places, and the BBC Club staff and cleaners – hope we weren't too untidy.

The singers, musicians, the DJs and promoters.

The wonderful armed forces for their support, and the police chums that used to pop into our rehearsal rooms for a cuppa, purely in the line of duty!

Those who left us too soon – Eric Morecambe and Ernie Wise, Ronnie Barker and John Denver.

Everyone who contributed their time and memories to the book: above all Sue and Lorelly of course, together with Ian Anderson, Robert Powell, Bryan Showell, Paul Smith and Ed Stewart. Thanks too to Jonathan Rigby, plus all the members of panspeople.com and oneforthedads.

And not forgetting the fans, who remember us all these years later.

There are so many people to thank, and we're sorry if you haven't been mentioned. But we do think of you – and you all know who you are.

Babs would like to dedicate this book to her brother John, and Dee Dee to her twin brother Stuart.

OVERLEAF:
Dee Dee, Ruth, Flick, Babs, Andi and Louise in a promotional photo for Belgian television, 1968.

PHOTO CREDITS

Page: 2 BBC; 6 BBC; 8 John Powell; 10 Chris Bentley; 66 John Powell; 69 BBC; 70 Getty Images; 72 Paul Smith; 74 Paul Smith; 79 Getty Images; 82 Frazer Wood; 86 Getty Images; 88 Getty Images; 90 Getty Images; 93 John Powell; 108 Getty Images; 133 Richard Imrie; 134 BBC; 138 John Powell; 141 BBC; 142 Getty Images; 145 BBC; 147 BBC; 150 John Powell; 153 Getty Images; 162 John Powell; 171 Getty Images; 172 Getty Images; 174 John Powell; 177 John Powell; 178 BBC; 183 Getty Images; 188 BBC; 191 BBC; 197 Getty Images; 207 *Punch* magazine; 201 Danjaq LLC and United Artists Corporation; 214 John Powell. All other images courtesy The Pan's People Collection.

Colour section
Page: 1 John Powell; 2 (top) Paul Smith; (bottom) Getty Images; 2-3 Getty Images; 4 (top) BBC; (bottom) Getty Images; 5 BBC; 6 Getty Images; 7 (top) Getty Images; (bottom) BBC; 8 John Powell.

Front cover and front flap: John Powell. Back cover: BBC.

Every effort has been made to trace the copyright holders of images in this book and we apologise for any errors and omissions. Any corrections will be incorporated in future reprints or editions.